—— WALKER'S COMPANION ——

PEAK DISTRICT

WALKER'S COMPANION

PEAK DISTRICT

JOHN AND ANNE NUTTALL

Photography by John Heseltine

TED SMART

ACKNOWLEDGMENTS

We want to record our appreciation of the many people who have helped us during the writing of this book. First of all thank you to Roland Smith and Andrew Greenwood of the Peak Park Board who checked the manuscript. During the walks wet met and talked with many of the full-time and part-time Peak District rangers. Mr Geoff Frost, Mr Brian Jones, Mr Tony Hood, Mrs Margaret Bailey, and their colleagues were very informative and most helpful. We would also like to thank Mr Peter Gray, the Chairman of the Derbyshire and Lancashire Gliding Club; Mr Dave Wilson of the National Trust, who checked our list of routes; Mr A. F. Roberts and Mr J. R. Leach, authors of *The Coal Mines of Buxton*; and Alan and Hilda Mitchell for their help on the section on farming. We thank the following for permission to use material from their publications: The Peak Park Joint Planning Board ('Access to Open Country') and the Countryside Commission ('The Countryside Access Charter'). The maps were drawn from the Outdoor Leisure and Pathfinder maps of the area with the permission of the Ordnance Survey. Thank you also to our two sons, Jeremy and Joseph, who have put up with their parents' obsession. Finally thank you to Mark Richards who gave us the opportunity of writing this book. We've enjoyed every minute of it.

This edition produced for
The Book People Ltd,
Hall Wood Avenue,
Haydock,
St Helens WA11 9UL

First published in 1994 by Ward Lock

This book is based on material originally published in the *Great Walks* series.

Printed and bound in Spain by Graficromo S.A.,Cordoba

ISBN 0-7063-7247-6

CONTENTS

INTRODUCTION

During the writing of this book we have visited and revisited many familiar parts of the Peak District. Yet every time there is something new to see, to hear and to experience. Whether it has been wandering along Stanage Edge under a cloudless blue sky, or returning by moonlight down Alport Dale or even groping our way by compass off Bleaklow in mist and rain, we have enjoyed it all.

In an area with so much to offer, the choice of the best walks is never easy as it always means leaving something out. After much deliberation there were still places which we wanted to include and there was always the temptation to make every walk just that little bit longer to get something special in; but in the end, in our opinion, this selection gives the finest of the Peak District walks. They vary considerably in length and difficulty, so there should be something to suit everyone's inclination and the time available.

Each walk has a route description followed by information on things to see along the way. John Heseltine has captured the spirit and special quality of the Peak District in his excellent photographs.

The White Peak and the Dark Peak cover a fascinating area which is within only a few miles of nearly half the population of England. Sometimes, close to Sheffield on a sunny Sunday, it can indeed be crowded; yet on many occasions we have walked for hours without meeting another person. But it is not always good weather! The wild moors can be very wild indeed and in bad weather to the unwary or ill prepared they can be savage and unforgiving of a mistake.

However, even though warm sun and blue skies make excellent weather for walking, the less good conditions are often just as enjoyable and sometimes far more memorable. To be on the high moors when the sun breaks through the swirling clouds, or to climb out of the valley mist to find the tops clear and the valley bottom filled with white rivers of fog, or to crunch your way over the iron-hard, frozen peat, these are the moments that will live for ever.

THE PEAK DISTRICT
NATIONAL PARK

National Parks are areas of country with exceptionally attractive scenery that are specially protected.

The purpose of a National Park is to protect the more attractive parts of the country from being spoilt and to set aside areas for people who live in towns and cities to enjoy open air recreation. In Britain the title National Park is misleading as it is not a park in the urban sense, neither is it owned by the nation. The Parks, unlike many National Parks abroad, are not undeveloped wildernesses. The Peak Park, although sparsely inhabited in comparison with the surrounding heartland of industrial Britain, is home to many people and its 'unspoilt' scenery owes much to the activity of man. Most of the land in fact belongs to private farmers and landowners. Although much of Britain is under private ownership, which makes public access difficult, in the National Parks there is generally freer access to open country than elsewhere, either by custom, as in the Lake District, or by formal Access Agreements with the landowners. The latter covers large areas of Peak District open moorland.

In 1935 the Council for the Preservation of Rural England set up a Standing Committee for National Parks. The National Parks and Access to the Countryside Act of 1949 was responsible for the creation of each individual Park in England and Wales. Eleven National Parks have so far been established. The Countryside Commission took over responsibility for the Parks in 1968 and, in 1974, an administrative authority was set up in each Park.

The National Park Authorities are responsible for conservation, the control of development and the provision of facilities for visitors. They try to combine support for the local economy with conservation and provision for recreation.

Since 1974 the Peak District National Park has been managed by a Joint Planning Board. This has a technical department at Bakewell and devotes its attention to the special problems of the Peak District. It has 34 members, of whom 23 are appointed by the County and District Councils having territory in the National Park, and 11 by the Secretary of State for the

Environment, who are chosen for their special knowledge of some aspect of the work of the Park.

Peak Park Information Centres which advise visitors are at:

Bakewell; Old Market Hall *Bakewell* (0629) 813227
Castleton; Castle Street *Hope Valley* (0443) 620679
Edale; Fieldhead *Hope Valley* (0443) 670207
Fairholmes; Upper Derwent Valley *Hope Valley* (0443) 650953
Torside; Longdendale Valley
Hartington; Hartington Old Station
Langsett, Langsett Barn

The opening times of the information centres vary, some are not open in the winter.

SOME FACTS AND FIGURES ABOUT THE PEAK DISTRICT NATIONAL PARK

DESIGNATED Designation confirmed in April 1951. The Peak District was the first National Park in Great Britain.

AREA 555 sq miles (143 800 hectares). This covers a large amount of Derbyshire plus adjoining parts of Staffordshire, Cheshire, Greater Manchester, and West and South Yorkshire. The greatest length north to south is nearly 40 miles (65 km), and the greatest breadth about 24 miles (39 km). The long central slice of land excluded from the park is industrial and includes the towns of New Mills, Whaley Bridge, Chapel en le Frith and Buxton. Matlock and Darley Dale are also omitted.

EMBLEM A locally quarried millstone. These will be seen beside many of the roads leading into the park.

POPULATION Nearly 40 000 people live and work in the area of the Park. The principal town is Bakewell with about 4 000 inhabitants.

TOURISTS About 17 million people live within 60 miles (95 km) of its boundary. The Park can be approached from all directions and is frequented all year by people from the nearby industrial centres. Around 22 million day visitors come each year.

FINANCE This is derived mainly from the government with a smaller sum from the ratepayers, each one of whom pays less than the cost of a first class stamp in support for all 11 Parks. The Park earns 30% of its income through its own activities.

LAND OWNERSHIP Most of the land in the Park is privately owned. Some is owned by public bodies like the water authorities, the National Trust and the National Park Authority, while other areas are specially managed nature reserves.

SELECTED WALKS IN THE PEAK DISTRICT NATIONAL PARK

Path leading down to Monsal Viaduct

INTRODUCTION TO THE
ROUTE DESCRIPTIONS

1. ACCESS (see page 124)   All of the walks described in this book follow public rights-of-way, concessionary paths or are on access land. Please do not take short cuts that may annoy local people. Occasionally some of the access land which is grouse moor may be closed during the shooting season (see page 124).

2. ASCENT   The amount of climbing has been calculated from the Outdoor Leisure or appropriate Pathfinder map and is only approximate.

3. CAR-PARKS   Three-quarters of the walks start from a public car-park. The rest start from a lay-by or a wide part of a public road, but

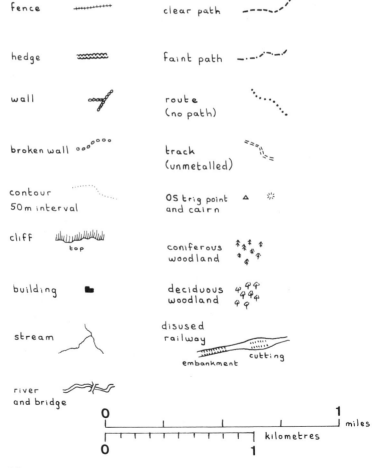

FIGURE 1 Signs used on detailed route maps

10

please take care when parking so as not to inconvenience others. Field gateways in particular should not be obstructed.

4. INTERESTING FEATURES
These are marked on the map and in the text by corresponding numbers, e.g. *(1)*, *(2)*, showing where they can best be seen.

5. LENGTH
Distances are in 'map miles', calculated from the relevant OS maps, with no account taken of ascent or descent.

6. MAPS
These are drawn to a scale of 1:25 000 using the symbols shown in fig. 1. Certain features have been exaggerated and others simplified to make them easier to read. Apart from the north-eastern edges, all the walks are covered by either the Dark Peak or White Peak maps in the Outdoor Leisure series. The north-eastern edges are on sheet SK 28/38. (The whole area is also covered by the Peak District Tourist Map.) The names used are those appearing on these OS maps. The arrow on the maps is grid north and the appropriate sheets of the OS Landranger and Outdoor Leisure maps are shown on each map. In most cases the maps have been drawn so that the route goes from the bottom to the top of each page.

7. ROUTE DESCRIPTION
The following abbreviations are used:

L and R: left and right. Where these are used for changes of direction then they imply a turn of about 90° when facing in the direction of the walk. 'Half L' and 'half R' indicate a half-turn, i.e. approximately 45°.

PFS: Public Footpath Sign
PBS: Public Bridleway Sign
PWS: Pennine Way Sign
OS: Ordnance Survey

To avoid constant repetition, it should be assumed that all stiles and gates mentioned in the route description are to be crossed (unless there is a specific statement otherwise).

8. STANDARD OF THE ROUTES
The routes in this book cover a wide range of difficulty; from those which are within the capabilities of the youngest and oldest, to those which are only for tough and experienced walkers. However, it should be remembered that much of the land in the Peak District National Park is at an altitude of over 1000 ft (305 m), and on the high moors up to 2000 ft (610 m), and thus in bad weather the conditions can deteriorate very rapidly. While the weather in the surrounding low-lying areas can be quite pleasant, on the moors it can be misty, raining, or snowing, and a stiff valley breeze can become a raging gale higher up. In winter also the roads in the Peak District frequently become blocked with snowdrifts; there are signs giving the road conditions over the passes, but it is still easy to become marooned.

Edale – the start of the Pennine Way

The routes have been graded from easiest to hardest, taking into account the distance and height climbed as well as the difficulty of the terrain, as follows.

Easy (1) Walks of less than 6 miles (10 km), with no more than 1000 ft (300 m) of ascent, and which mostly stay on paths. The paths may go near cliffs or steep drops so that care is needed, and if the weather should deteriorate, paths that cross high open moors can be rather exposed.

Moderate (2) Longer walks up to 10 miles (16 km), some climbing to around 2000 ft (610 m) on exposed moorland where there is not always a clearly defined path, so care and compass work is necessary in bad weather.

More strenuous (3) From 10 miles (16 km) in length, some with rough walking over moorland. Route-finding ability is required, especially in bad weather.

Very strenuous (4) Long, rough and tough moorland walking, only suitable for the very experienced hill-goer.

Each walk commences with a description of the area, and details of the distance covered and height climbed, together with any special difficulties which may be met.

9. WEATHER FORECAST   Local weather forecasts can be obtained from British Telecom's Weatherline.

12

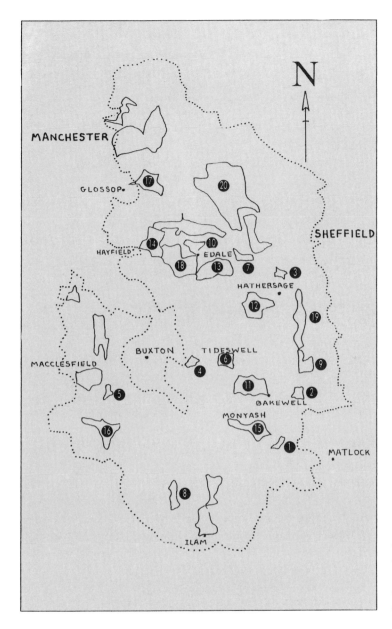

MANCHESTER

GLOSSOP

SHEFFIELD

HAYFIELD

EDALE

HATHERSAGE

BUXTON TIDESWELL

MACCLESFIELD

BAKEWELL

MONYASH

MATLOCK

ILAM

FIGURE 2 The Peak District National Park. The routes described have been marked on and numbered.

All the walks are circular. The number of the appropriate Landranger (1:50 000) map with a six figure grid reference (see page 125) is given for the location of the starting and finishing point of each walk. A sketch map (fig. 2) shows the location of each walk within the Park.

10. STARTING AND FINISHING POINTS

To estimate the length of time needed to complete a walk, fit walkers may use Naithsmith's formula, which is 3 miles (5 km) per hour plus one hour for every 2000 ft (610 m) of ascent. However, this does not allow for rests, food stops, photography, bad weather or difficulty of terrain, and most people will find that they have to allow more time than this for the walks.

11. TIME FOR COMPLETION

1·1

STANTON MOOR

STARTING AND
FINISHING POINT
Birchover. Cars
may be parked with
care in the village
(119-238622).

LENGTH
3 miles (5 km)

ASCENT
300 ft (90 m)

This small, attractive, heathery moor is covered with the evidence of past civilizations, including many stone circles and burial mounds. There are several interesting rocks, boulders and quarries to be seen, but please take care near the quarry edges.

ROUTE DESCRIPTION (Map 1)

Walk up the main street to a gate on the R (marked 'Barn Farm') at the end of the houses, opposite Ann Twyfords quarry *(1)*. Go up the farm road and to the R of the farm to a stile. Keep to the L of the fence to the gate and in the far corner of the next field a stile leads to a fenced path. At the end of the path turn half R over the stile, through the wall ahead at a gap and up to join the road at a stile in the hedge. Go L on the road for a few yards and turn R by the National Trust sign.

A fence follows the edge of Stanton Moor *(2)* for ½ mile (800 m) before turning L at the large inscribed boulder (EIN 1831) in which footholds have been cut. After 150 yards (135 m), cross the fence at a stile behind the tower *(3)*. Go half R on the path which, in 200 yards (180 m), reaches Nine Ladies Stone Circle among the trees. Turn L and cross the open moorland for ½ mile (800 m) on a clear path. Turn R at the junction. Passing the Cork Stone, which can be ascended by means of metal rungs, the road is reached in ¼ mile (400 m). Turn L and just before the road turns L, go through a gap on the R and descend through the woods to the Druid Inn with Rowter Rocks *(4)* behind. Turn L back into Birchover.

1 Ann Twyfords Quarry
This is one of the few quarries still producing traditional millstones. They also manufacture grindstones which are used in engineering works, in glass bevelling and for knife sharpening. Large stones from the quarry are used in the manufacture of paper in crushing the wood to pulp and of course a lot of building stone is also produced.

Opposite
Stanton Moor

14

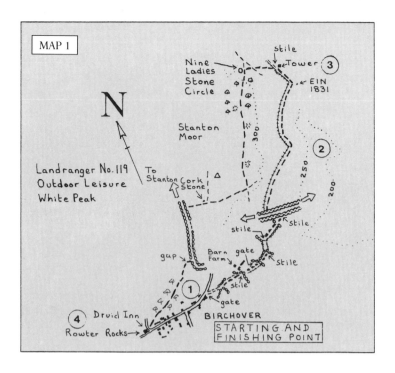

MAP 1

N

Landranger No. 119
Outdoor Leisure
White Peak

Nine Ladies Stone Circle

Stanton Moor

To Stanton Cork Stone

stile

Tower ③

EIN 1831

②

300

250

200

stile

stile

gap

Barn gate
Farm

stile

stile

① stile

gate

④ Druid Inn

Rowter Rocks→

BIRCHOVER

STARTING AND
FINISHING POINT

2 *Stanton Moor*

On the eastern edge of the Peak District limestone, this outcrop of sandstone holds in its 150 acres (60 hectares) of heather-clad moorland one of the finest collections of Bronze Age remains to be found in the British Isles. Over seventy barrows are scattered across the moor, with examples of stone circles, cairns and standing stones; the best preserved is the Nine Ladies Stone Circle, 33 ft (10 m) in diameter, with its King Stone close by. This was once enclosed by a stone wall which has now been removed. A private museum at Birchover was established by J. and J.P. Heathcote, who from 1927 to 1950 excavated seventy cairns on the moor. Twenty-seven acres (11 hectares) of the moor were gifted to the National Trust in 1934.

3 *Tower*

At one time an inscription over the door read 'Earl Grey 1832' in tribute to the gentleman who carried the Reform Bill through parliament.

4 *Rowter Rocks*

This fascinating maze of caves, stairs and tunnels in the rocks is a delight to explore. Once thought to have connections with Druid culture, it was in fact the work of the local vicar, Thomas Eyre (died 1717), who built a study among the rocks and carved rooms, armchairs and alcoves. A rocking stone here was unseated by vandals – not recently however; it was the work of a group of fourteen young men in 1799.

1·2

EDENSOR AND CHATSWORTH PARK

Although this walk follows public rights-of-way, a large part of the Chatsworth Estate is in fact freely open to the public to wander at will by the courtesy of the Duke and Duchess of Devonshire. Edensor village is a most charming place, while a visit to Chatsworth itself would complete a very pleasant day out.

STARTING AND
FINISHING POINT
Calton Lees car-park just off B6012, Beeley–Baslow road (119-259684).

LENGTH
4 miles (6.5 km)

ASCENT
400 ft (120 m)

ROUTE DESCRIPTION (Map 2)

From the car-park beside the B6012 walk towards the garden centre, through a gate ('No Thro' Road'), and follow the road round the bend to the track junction by Calton Lees Farm. Go

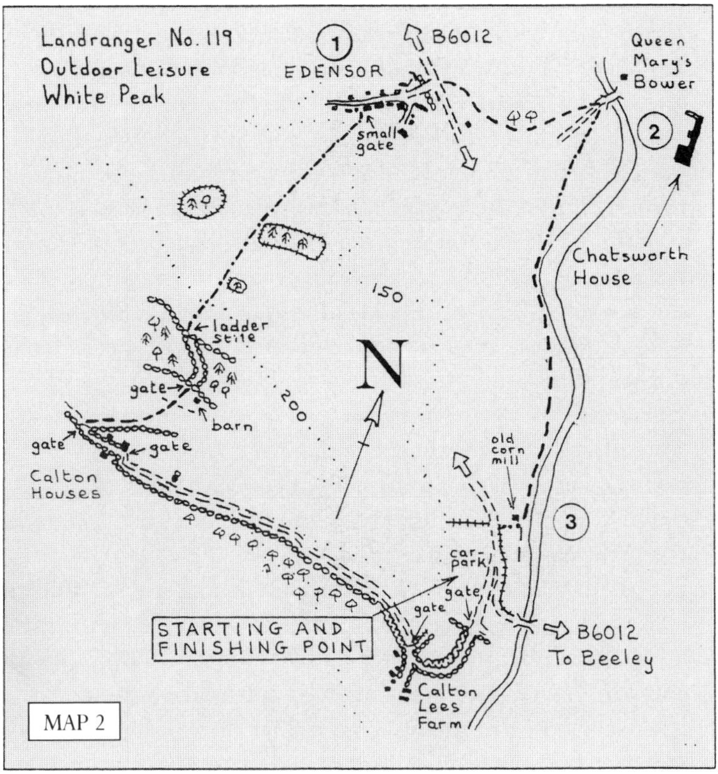

Landranger No. 119
Outdoor Leisure
White Peak

EDENSOR

① B6012

Queen Mary's Bower

small gate

②

150

Chatsworth House

ladder stile

gate

200

barn

gate   gate

Calton Houses

old corn mill

car-park

③

gate
gate

STARTING AND FINISHING POINT

B6012
To Beeley

Calton Lees Farm

N

MAP 2

straight across through the gate and follow the track for ¾ mile (1·2 km) to Calton Houses. The track goes through a gate, between buildings, and out into the field at a gate. Turn R and the path leads across the field and into the wood at a gate to the L of a barn. To the R is Russian Cottage, named from the friendship between the sixth Duke of Devonshire and the Czar.

Emerging over a ladder stile into Chatsworth Park, aim just L of the spire of Edensor Church and cross the parkland. Enter Edensor *(1)* at a small gate and some steps by the church, and turn R past the fine stone cottages. Cross the B6012 to the gravel path opposite which climbs through a stand of beech trees with a good view of Chatsworth *(2)* ahead. Descend to the bridge and turn R to follow the river for a mile (1·6 km) to the old corn mill *(3)*. Climb up the bank and cross the road to the car-park.

1 Edensor

Pronounced 'Ensor', the present village is of very recent origin. In 1755 the views from Chatsworth were improved by the demolition of all that could be seen of the old village. In 1839 the rest of the village, although hidden in the valley bottom, was also demolished with the single exception of a cottage which still stands today isolated on the other side of the road. The new village was designed by Sir Joseph Paxton (of Crystal Palace fame), and the church of St Peter, consecrated in 1866, was the work of Sir Gilbert Scott. The past Dukes of Devonshire and their families lie in a quiet corner of the churchyard, but visitors come here to visit another grave, that of Kathleen Kennedy, daughter of Joseph Kennedy, United States Ambassador to Britain and sister of the late John Kennedy, President of the United States, whose visit on 29 June 1963 is commemorated on a plaque in front of the grave.

2 Chatsworth

This magnificent mansion is principally the creation of the first Duke of Devonshire who between 1686 and 1707 practically rebuilt the original house piecemeal and also built the great cascade in the grounds.

The first house on this site was built in 1552 by Sir William Cavendish and his celebrated wife, Bess of Hardwick. The house faced east and the Cavendish Hunting Tower, which dates from this time, remains in its splendid position on the hillside above the house. Queen Mary's Bower, a kind of summer house near the bridge and dating from the same

Opposite
Chatsworth House

Edensor churchyard

time, encloses an ancient earthwork and was frequented by Mary Queen of Scots when she was a prisoner at Chatsworth in the custody of the Earl of Shrewsbury, Bess of Hardwick's fourth husband. Mary was here on five occasions between 1570 and 1581.

In the time of the fourth Duke the grounds were extensively remodelled under the direction of Capability Brown, and new roads, which ran north–south, replaced the former east–west alignment. The sixth Duke added the famous Emperor Fountain which throws a jet of water 290 ft (90 m) into the air, which when built was the second highest fountain in the world.

The house itself contains a splendid collection of treasures, paintings, tapestries, sculptures and other works of art, and in the grounds there are large herds of fallow deer.

Old Corn Mill

This mill, built about 1760 in a style complementary to Chatsworth House, was in operation, grinding corn, until 1950. A millstone still leans against an outer wall. During a gale in 1962 the building was badly damaged when trees fell on it, and now only the shell remains by the side of the River Derwent.

20

1·3

STANAGE EDGE

Stanage is the most popular gritstone climbing edge in the Peak District. Within easy reach of Sheffield, the rocks attract climbers every weekend and during the summer evenings. At one time millstones were quarried here and piles of them may still be seen below the edge stacked on end awaiting the collection that will never come.

The visit to the old guidepost of Stanedge Pole may be omitted thus shortening the walk to 3 miles (5 km).

ROUTE DESCRIPTION (Map 3)

Walk up the main track and when it bends R by a small plantation go over the stile on the L. Climb the slope towards High Neb to meet a path near a large boulder. Turn R for a few yards and then up to the boulder which has several large millstones *(1)* beside it. A small path through the bracken then leads up to the rocks, passing more stacked millstones. At the foot of the rocks turn L and scramble up the heathery slopes to the path on the top of the rocks with the OS trig point of High Neb just to the L. Close by, there is a hollow in the rock identified by the number 9; about a hundred numbered basins like this can be found across the moor. These were carved at the beginning of the twentieth century by two gamekeepers to provide drinking water for the grouse. Hollow number 8 can be found on the jutting prow of rock nearby which is a good vantage point. On the top turn R. Walking back along Stanage Edge *(2)*, a useful shelter has been built a short distance off the path to the L. In ½ mile (800 m) a stile is crossed. When the main track comes in from the R, carry on along this to the boundary of open country.

The shorter variant now stays by the edge to join the return route which descends the edge by a paved trackway. The longer route goes half L keeping by the fence following the Long Causeway to Stanedge Pole *(3)*. Beyond the pole is Redmires Reservoir and to the L is Stanedge Lodge. Head now to the R

STARTING AND FINISHING POINT
Car-park by Dennis Knoll beneath Stanage Edge, north of Hathersage (110-227843).

LENGTH
4½ miles (7 km) or 3 miles (5 km) variant

ASCENT
500 ft (150 m)

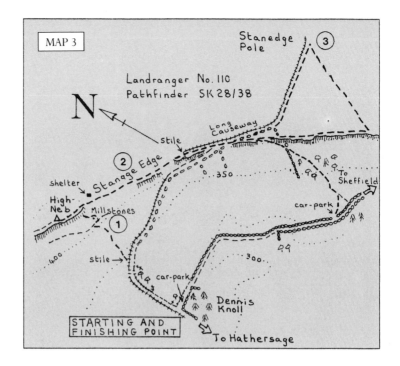

MAP 3

Stanedge Pole ③

Landranger No. 110
Pathfinder SK 28/38

N

stile

Long Causeway

② Stanage Edge

shelter

High-Neb

Millstones

350

To Sheffield

car-park

①

400

stile →

300

car-park

Dennis Knoll

STARTING AND
FINISHING POINT

To Hathersage

back towards the edge; this path can be rather boggy in its middle section. At the edge turn R and in ½ mile (800 m), by a prominent boulder, the paved descent route is reached (also the shorter variant). This leads pleasantly downhill to Stanage Plantation passing the 'Grand Hotel', a gigantic fallen block with a bivouac cave beneath it. Beyond the wood fork R down to a car-park and into a lane. Turn R back to the start 1 mile (1·6 km) along the road.

1 Millstones

Piles of millstones lie beneath Stanage Edge; some of them flawed, but most of them stacked ready, then abandoned. From early Norman times gritstone has been used in corn milling, while Sheffield's cutlery and steel industry was founded on the proximity of the millstone grit which provided the grindstones.

The stones, which at Stanage were dug from the ground and in other places quarried, are of several different forms and sizes. The earliest ones are thinner, about 12 in (30 cm) deep at the centre tapering towards the outer edge, and 6–7 ft (1.8–2.1 m) in diameter. The Stanage stones are usually of a later type, from 3–7 ft (0.9–2.1 m) diameter, cylindrical and somewhat thicker. The stones were first cut to a hexagon and then trimmed to a circular shape while standing on a stone pedestal. They were next flattened on both sides and lastly the central hole was made. As the stones would have been too

Opposite

Looking west from Long Causeway on Stanage Edge

22

heavy for transport by packhorses, sledges may have been used, or the stones may even have been rolled along. They were moved by waggons later.

The introduction of the superior French millstones in the mid-eighteenth century caused a dramatic fall in demand for the local product, which led the workers to riot, smashing the foreign stones in the mills. However by 1862, with the coming of the first roller mills, the end of the trade was in sight.

2 *Stanage Edge*

Probably the most popular climbers' crag in the Peak District, Stanage Edge is nearly 3 miles (5 km) in length with over 500 routes of all standards of difficulty. The earliest explorer of the delights of Stanage climbing was J.W. Puttrell who paid his first visit in 1890, pioneering several gully routes which are still climbed today. The greatest single advance in standards at Stanage was achieved in the 1950s by the legendary Joe Brown and the late Don Whillans; but standards never stay still and new and harder routes are still being produced on what may only be an outcrop, but which to its many devotees is as fine as many a mountain anywhere.

3 *Stanedge Pole*

Erected at a height of 1453 ft (443 m) on the Hallam moors, this was a landmark for jaggers leading packhorse trains. The pole, now encircled by protective iron bands, directed them on the route from Sheffield to Stanage Edge by way of the Long Causeway. A beautifully paved track which passes over the edge at the easiest point and slopes gently downhill to the plantation beyond is more recent and was probably built for the carriage of millstones. The pole is known to have been there in 1550, as this date is carved on the rock at its foot. Parish road surveyors who renewed it every fifty years have also carved their names on the rock.

1·4

CHEE DALE

Kingfishers and dippers skim the waters of the River Wye, which is crossed and recrossed many times by the huge arches of the disused Midland railway as it follows this narrow limestone valley. The old railway track is followed for a short way past the impressive cliffs of Plum Buttress, before descending to the river. At two places the path follows stepping stones in the river and after heavy rain these may become impassable, and you will have to retrace your steps. Therefore this walk is best kept for dryish conditions.

STARTING AND FINISHING POINT Car-park on A6, Buxton–Bakewell road. Opposite Topley Pike Quarry (119-104725).

LENGTH
4½ miles (7 km)

ASCENT
500 ft (150 m)

ROUTE DESCRIPTION (Map 4)

Follow the track beside the river away from the A6 and under two of the railway arches. In ½ mile (800 m), just before a third arch, turn R up some steps to join the disused railway (PFS 'Monsal Trail') *(1)*. Turn R on the railway past Plum Buttress *(2)* which towers above on the R. At the next bridge over the river turn L down a little path to the river (sign 'Chee Dale'). Cross the footbridge and turn R down steps to the river-bank. Soon

The River Wye, Chee Dale

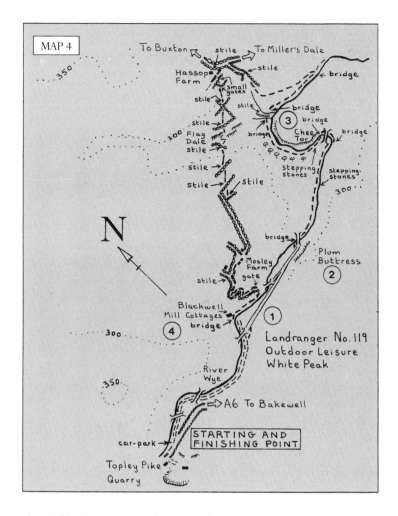

To Buxton stile To Miller's Dale
350
stile
Hassop bridge
Farm
small
gates
stile stile bridge
stile 3 bridge
Flag brige Chee bridge
Dale Tor
stile
stile Stepping stepping
stones stones
stile stile 300

N

bridge
Plum
Mosley Buttress
Farm
stile gate 2

Blackwell
Mill Cottages 1
300 4 bridge Landranger No.119
Outdoor Leisure
White Peak
River
Wye
350

A6 To Bakewell

STARTING AND
car-park FINISHING POINT

Topley Pike
Quarry

the cliffs close in, overhanging the river, and you take to the stepping stones. In ¼ mile (400 m) the river enters a gorge. Two footbridges allow the river to be crossed and recrossed by the Nature Reserve, bypassing the gorge. Again the cliffs close in and only the stepping stones allow further progress. The cliff beyond overhangs considerably, while opposite are the sheer cliffs of Chee Tor *(3)*, also popular with climbers. The foot of Flag Dale is reached, with two footbridges and a stile just before Wormhill Springs which gush forth from beside the path. The dale soon widens out and at an iron footbridge after ¼ mile (400 m), double back up the hillside.

The path, with a natural paving of bare limestone, climbs gradually up the hillside and then swings away from Chee Dale and up to a stile and walled track which leads to the road. Turn L beside the road for a few yards and then L (PFS 'Great Rocks') at a stile. Go through the farm to a very small gate in the wall, half R to a similar gate and down to a stile in the corner. Continue in the same line to a stile above Flag Dale and zig-zag

Opposite *Chee Dale from the Wormhill road*

26

down into the dale. Climb steeply out of the dale to a stile and go straight ahead across the field to an indistinct stile. The next stile is to the R of the overhead lines and then, in the corner of the field beyond, a stile leads to a walled lane. Turn L down to the farm and R at the barn. Passing the farm, where the farm track turns R, turn L at a stile and zig-zag down the hill to a gate and under the railway. Turn R and walk beside the river to Blackwell Mill Cottages *(4)* to cross the river at a footbridge. The car-park is just over ½ mile (800 m) back up the track.

1 The Monsal Trail

The Peak Park Board negotiated with British Rail for twelve years before an agreement was reached which allowed the track to be put to new use in 1981 as the Monsal Trail. BR provided £154000 towards the cost of repairs and although money is not yet available to improve the track surface in Chee Dale, making it rather rough walking on the old gravel ballast, it is a very attractive walk with spectacular views of the magnificent limestone cliffs.

The Buxton to Matlock railway, which reached Manchester in 1867, closed in 1968. The Great Rocks Dale to Doveholes section, however, is still in use, running through one of Europe's biggest quarries, principally for the supply of lime to the ICI works.

2 Plum Buttress

This is one of the finest limestone cliffs in the Peak District with several high standard climbs around 200 ft (60 m) in length, which ascend to the obvious horizontal slot, where the tiny figures of climbers will often be seen belayed. The routes then go over or around the overhanging face above.

3 Chee Tor

Another of Chee Dale's imposing limestone cliffs, whose most celebrated route is the Chee Tor Girdle. This, as its name indicates, traverses the cliff along the fault line, rather than, as is more usual with rock climbs, going straight up. This gives a rock climb of nearly 600 ft (180 m) in length, all of it exposed. The surrounding area is a Derbyshire Naturalist's Trust Nature Reserve.

4 Blackwell Mill Cottages

Surrounded by railway lines, these were built for railway workers and were serviced by a tiny railway station, Blackwell Halt, comprising one up and one down platform, each just long enough to take one carriage. The weir supplied Blackwell Mill, which has almost completely disappeared.

1·5

THREE SHIRE HEADS

The gritstone packhorse bridge at Three Shire Heads, where the counties of Derbyshire, Cheshire and Staffordshire meet, is not far from the road, but in a short walk you can feel very far away from the rush of the present day as you look down on Panniers Pool and think of the packhorse trains moving slowly through this countryside. In fact you are in the middle of a once industrial area which only recently has reverted to the wild state seen today.

The walk crosses the infant River Dane which in exceptionally wet weather can be difficult; if so, go out and back to Three Shire Heads by the return route.

STARTING AND
FINISHING POINT
Lay-by on A54
Congleton–Buxton
road near
Danebower
Quarries
(119-008699).

LENGTH
4½ miles (7 km) or
3 miles (5 km)
variant

ASCENT
700 ft (215 km)

ROUTE DESCRIPTION (Map 5)

A few yards from the lay-by, towards Buxton, take the track towards a chimney which is all that remains of the Dane Colliery. Go through a gate and follow the track through Danebower Quarries to the River Dane. Cross the river, turn R and follow the track up to Reeve-edge Quarries and continue beside the wall.

The view gradually opens out as the track veers L away from the River Dane. The moorland on the R, pitted with depressions, speaks of the industrial past of this area when coal was dug from many small mines. Shortly you come to Blackclough Farm on the R and then the path rounds the head of a clough, crossing an iron gate.

As the main track bends L immediately above a small cottage, leave it and take a descending minor track which leads in roughly the same direction. Just before an unusual T-shaped sheep shelter, the right-of-way doubles back. Aim for the cottage, turn L through the gateposts, and head directly downhill to pass through a tumbledown wall. At the field corner the path meets the road by the entrance to Blackclough Farm. Turn R and take the R fork following the stream. Go through an iron gate and very shortly take the L fork continuing to follow

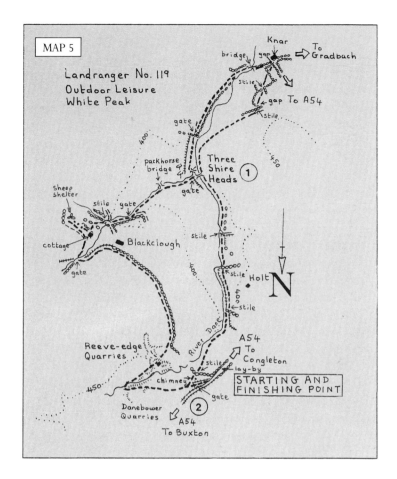

MAP 5

Landranger No. 119
Outdoor Leisure
White Peak

Knar
bridge   gap   To Gradbach
stile
gap To A54
stile
gate
oo
packhorse   Three
bridge   Shire
Heads ①
450
Sheep
shelter
stile   gate   gate
cottage   ■ Blackclough
stile
gate   stile   Holt   N
oo
stile
River Dane
Reeve-edge
Quarries   A54
stile   To
Congleton
450   chimney   lay-by
gate   STARTING AND
FINISHING POINT
Danebower
Quarries   ②
A54
To Buxton

the stream downhill, passing an interesting small packhorse bridge on the L, to reach Three Shire Heads *(1)* at a gate. The shorter variant now turns R over the bridge.

For the longer route do not cross the packhorse bridge ahead, but turn L and take the broad, sandy track which leads across another small bridge. Panniers Pool is the pool immediately below the bridges. In about 200 yards (180 m) pass through an iron gate and take the R fork along the wall. Follow the river until you come to a stout wooden bridge. Cross the bridge and climb up a steep track until Knar Farm is reached at a gate. Do not go through the gate, but turn immediately R onto a grassy track across the field. Go between gateposts at the next wall and then bear L up the hillside to a squeezer stile in the wall above. Turn R and follow the track rising gradually across the hillside through the next field and a small field beyond to emerge over a wooden stile onto a major track. Turn R and after a few yards a sandy track comes in from the L. This track leads gently downhill back to Three Shire Heads where the shorter route is rejoined.

Follow the River Dane upstream and at a five barred gate

Opposite
Reeve-edge Quarries

31

cross the stile on the R to stay by the river. Where the river turns R, cross a stile and the field below Holt Farm. As the river meanders back, follow the fence until it meets the wall, where a stile allows you to rejoin the river-bank. A little further on, the ruins of a mine building herald the Dane Colliery *(2)* which would go unnoticed if it were not for the chimney. The track now leads uphill and over a stile, with the chimney straight ahead. Go through the gate above to rejoin the path back to the main road.

1 Three Shire Heads

At this charming spot by Panniers Pool, four packhorse ways meet to cross the River Dane. The bridge, if examined underneath, will be seen to have been widened on the upstream side, indicating the importance of the crossing and the heavy traffic it must once have seen. A map of 1610 calls this Three Shire Stones.

Packhorse trains, that is strings of up to forty or even fifty horses, were the principal means used for the transport of goods from the Middle Ages until the seventeenth century. Because packhorses could travel over the moors so much more easily than waggons, packhorses were being used in the Peak District well into the nineteenth century. Over boggy ground these tracks were paved with gritstone slabs which often can still be seen. It was, of course, much cheaper to maintain a narrow packhorse track than one for waggons, and bridges could be made narrower too. The name jagger, which occurs in some placenames such as Jaggers Clough on Kinder, was applied to the leader of a packhorse train and comes from Jaeger-galloway, the breed of horse most in use in the Peak District. The packhorses carried many varied loads, one of the earliest being salt, hence the name saltways.

The nearby village of Flash, which at 1518 ft (460 m) above sea level is claimed to be the highest village in England, depended on trade via the packhorse routes as the land hereabouts is poor. However, the ease with which one could escape the law by crossing into an adjacent county at Three Shire Heads led to a certain notoriety for Flash, and its name was applied to the coining of 'flash', or counterfeit, money by the inhabitants.

2 Dane Colliery

The coal mines in the Buxton area were never on the scale of those in the main industrial areas, but before rail transport brought in cheap coal from outside, these mines were

important to the local community. Mining started at the *Knar* beginning of the seventeenth century and continued until as late as World War I, although the principal activity occurred in the period 1780 to 1880. The coal was used to burn limestone for use in mortar for building, and also in agriculture for improving the land.

The Blackclough Mine connected underground with the Dane Colliery. Dane Colliery produced some of the best and cleanest coal in the area; the coal of many other mines contained impurities such as sulphur and iron pyrites. The chimney, which is all that remains visible today, was connected by a flue running down the hillside to what was probably an engine house. The remains of the flue can still be seen in places. An opening near the river was the end of the sough or drainage level for the mine.

33

1·6

RAVENSDALE

STARTING AND
FINISHING POINT
Tideswell Dale
car-park
(119-153743).
1 mile (1.6 km)
south of Tideswell.

LENGTH
5½ miles (9 km)

ASCENT
650 ft (200 m)

This walk should ideally be done in summer when Ravensdale (Cressbrook Dale) displays one of the greatest profusion and variety of flowers to be found anywhere in the Peak District.

The walk starts in Tideswell Dale where a basalt quarry has been reclaimed by the Peak Park Board who have removed the old machinery and grassed over the spoil heaps to provide an attractive picnic spot. Part of the dale has been declared a Site of Special Scientific Interest (SSSI). The walk continues along Miller's Dale (whose limestone cliffs are popular with rock climbers) down to Cressbrook Mill, and then Ravensdale is followed to the village of Litton.

ROUTE DESCRIPTION (Map 6)

From the car-park take the track down Tideswell Dale. At the Y fork, branch R down the dale and at the next junction also fork R. Just before reaching the road, Tideswell Dale Cave is passed on the L close to the path. This is an old resurgence cave with a 100 ft (30 m) passage leading to a small chamber.

Join the road, turn L and follow the River Wye to reach Litton Mill *(1)* in about 200 yards (180 m). A concessionary path leads through the old factory and down beside the river. After a

Tideswell Dale

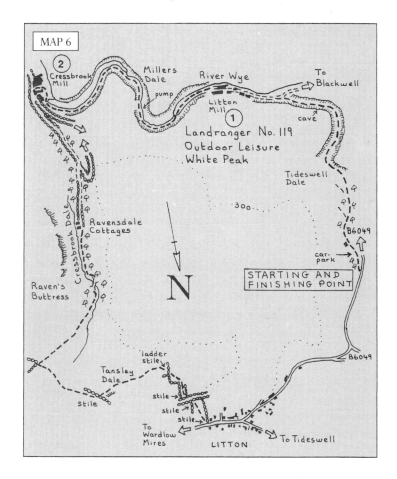

MAP 6

② Cressbrook Mill

Millers Dale

River Wye

To Blackwell

pump

Litton Mill

① cave

Landranger No. 119
Outdoor Leisure
White Peak

Tideswell Dale

300

B6049

Ravensdale Cottages

Cressbrook Dale

Raven's Buttress

car-park

N

STARTING AND
FINISHING POINT

B6049

ladder stile

Tansley Dale

stile →

stile

stile →

stile →

To Wardlow Mires

LITTON

To Tideswell

short while you will pass a small ruined waterwheel; this was once used to pump drinking water from a spring up to Cressbrook village above. Passing a swampy section of the river, the disused railway line to Bakewell and Derby may be seen where it emerges briefly from one of the tunnels at the top of a steep embankment beautifully constructed of limestone blocks. The river widens out to form a millpond, and at the end of this cross the leat by the bridge into the grounds of Cressbrook Mill *(2)*.

Emerging onto the road, turn L and immediately take the R fork, (sign 'Cressbrook and Litton'). Follow the road uphill under its canopy of trees and turn R (sign 'Ravensdale No Through Road') to the charming Ravensdale Cottages, built originally for mill workers. High above the trees on the opposite side of Ravensdale is Raven's Buttress whose limestone cliffs reach over 150 ft (45 m) in height. Take the narrow path straight ahead to the L of the cottage gardens.

Ravensdale is a 'dry' valley with a stream only during the wetter months. The path crosses a plank bridge and then forks. Take the clearer uphill path and, on reaching the valley rim, descend again to the L past grassed-over spoil tips of the old lead mines. Cross the wall at a wooden stile to follow Tansley Dale opposite (i.e. branching away from the main dale).

At the top of Tansley Dale a flight of steps leads up to a ladder stile. Cross this and head diagonally uphill to the wall corner ahead and to a stile onto a lane. Turn L and in a few yards clamber over the stile at the wall corner. Cross the field to the opposite corner, over the stone step stile onto the road, and turn L into Litton (meaning 'farm on a hill'), passing a cottage which dates from 1639. Hammerton Hall Farm is somewhat later in date, with 1768 picked out at the top of the rainwater down pipes. On the opposite side of the road, outside the Red Lion, are the village stocks, and close by is a gritstone cross. Take the road signposted 'Tideswell and Miller's Dale'.

At the T-junction onto the B6049, turn L onto this 1812 turnpike road. After ½ mile (800 m) a stand of fine mature beech trees on the L marks a footpath which leads back to the car-park.

1 *Litton Mill*

This mill, opened in 1782 for cotton spinning, was notorious for the exploitation of its workforce of apprentices imported from the London poorhouses. In an age when long hours and hard labour for children were common, Litton Mill's conditions, food and treatment were exceptionally bad, leading to the death of so many that burials were not conducted locally in order to avoid scandal. Most of the present buildings are late nineteenth century, and from 1934 until 1963 the mill produced silk and later man-made fibres.

2 *Cressbrook Mill*

The first mill, built around 1783, was destroyed by fire only two years later, but was promptly rebuilt and used for cotton weaving. The present building, now looking sadly dilapidated, dates from 1815 and was in use as a cotton mill until 1965. Although London apprentices were also employed here, the conditions were relatively better than at Litton Mill; the children worked six days a week and actually had a few hours off on a Sunday! Dale Terrace, the row of houses on the north side of the mill, was originally called Apprentices Row. The Gothic section at the end was probably a chapel.

The millpond dominates and fills the valley above the mill, and the footpath squeezes past it under overhanging limestone cliffs. There is a smaller millpond at the foot of Ravensdale on the opposite side of the road.

Opposite *Woods at Tideswell Dale*

1·7

WIN HILL FROM YORKSHIRE BRIDGE

STARTING AND
FINISHING POINT
Yorkshire Bridge
off A6013, south of
Ladybower
Reservoir
(110-198850).

LENGTH
5 miles (8 km)

ASCENT
1000 ft (300 m)

Like its twin summit of Lose Hill across the Hope Valley, Win
Hill is at the end of a ridge. Kinder throws down a long narrow
spur towards the Ladybower Reservoir and the last outpost
before the plunge into the valley is this splendid rocky summit.
The initial ascent is very steep, but it is on a good path and once
over the rest of the walk is nearly all downhill. The trees beside
Ladybower Reservoir look particularly attractive in their
autumn colours.

ROUTE DESCRIPTION (Map 7)

From the bridge walk up towards Ladybower Reservoir *(1)* for a
few yards and over the stile beside the gate. Turn L up the steps
and cross the track of the old railway line *(2)* built during the
construction of the Howden and Derwent Reservoirs. A stile
marks the start of the ascent through the woods beside the
stream, which for ¼ mile (400 m) is very steep indeed. When a
track crosses the path, the angle eases and shortly a stile is
crossed at a walled track. Go through the gap opposite and carry
on uphill. Soon the trees are left behind and the open heather-
clad moorland is reached. A ladder stile is crossed and the
summit rocks of Win Hill *(3)* are only a short climb ahead.

Take in the view from the summit of Win Hill. To the north
are the twin fingers of the Ladybower Reservoir, the Woodlands
Valley, which runs west, and the Derwent Valley, which runs
north up into the hills. From the fine rocky summit the path
sets off westwards over the moorland following the broad ridge
to meet and follow a wall for a short distance. To the L the
Great Ridge, culminating in Lose Hill, is seen end on. The path
then turns north-west, still following the ridge, until a wall is
reached. Turn R on the far side and in a few yards enter the
forest at a gap in the wall. Follow the forest track as it bends L
and then R down to a major junction. Go straight across on the
now minor grassy track and then L to descend to meet the
Ladybower Reservoir.

38

Turn R on the track which follows the attractively wooded *Woods above* shores of the reservoir for about 2 miles (3 km), finally passing *Ladybower* the dam. The road then leads downhill back to the stile by Yorkshire Bridge. This bridge into Yorkshire was first recorded in 1599.

1 *Ladybower Reservoir*
Early plans were for several small reservoirs at the junction of the Ashop and Derwent Valleys; but this large one was eventually begun in 1935 and drowned the village of Derwent under the vast expanse of 6300 million gallons of water behind the massive dam at Bamford. Unlike the other two dams in the valley, Ladybower Dam is constructed with an earth embankment and clay core. Water is prevented from undermining the dam by concrete filled boreholes and a deep trench beneath the base of the dam. Ladybower Reservoir was completed in 1943 despite wartime difficulties with materials. It was opened by King George VI in September 1945 and took two years to fill. The dam is 1250 ft (380 m) long and 140 ft (45 m) high. At its base it is 665 ft (200 m)

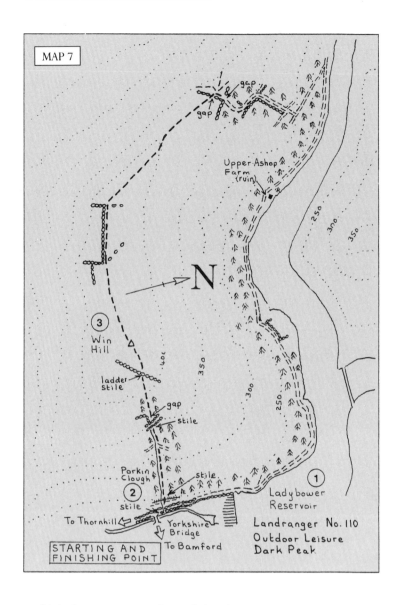

MAP 7

Upper Ashop Farm (ruin)

N

③ Win Hill

ladder stile

gap

stile

Parkin Clough

② stile

stile

To Thornhill

Yorkshire Bridge

To Bamford

STARTING AND FINISHING POINT

① Ladybower Reservoir

Landranger No. 110
Outdoor Leisure
Dark Peak

thick, but tapers to only 17 ft (5 m) at the top.

2 *Old Railway*
See Derwent and Howden Reservoirs (page 121).

3 *Win Hill*
The summit at 1516 ft (462 m) was, according to legend, the camp of King Edwin of Northumbria who fought a bloody battle in the Hope Valley below against Cuicholm, the King of Wessex. The hill where King Cuicholm had made his camp became known as Lose Hill and the victorious King Edwin's campsite was known as Win Hill. It is more likely that 'win' refers to bilberries, while 'lose' is an old name for pigs.

Opposite *The summit of Win Hill*

40

1·8

THE MANIFOLD VALLEY

STARTING AND
FINISHING POINT
Car-park at
Wetton Mill near
Butterton
(119-095561).

LENGTH
5½ miles (9 km)

ASCENT
900 ft (280 m)

The Manifold Valley has, like its more famous sister Dovedale, limestone caverns and cliffs. However, as well as being usually much quieter it also has a disappearing river, Thor's Cave, which is in fact bigger than any in Dovedale and a veritable honeycomb of disused shafts and levels in the copper mines of Ecton Hill.

ROUTE DESCRIPTION (Map 8)

From the car-park, go over the bridge and L up the road to Dale Farm. Go through the farmyard to the L of the farmhouse, under the pipes ('Headroom 5 ft 8 in') and through the gate to walk up the dale. Continue until you come immediately below the Sugarloaf, a steep, limestone reef knoll, and skirt it to the L on a small path which climbs to a PFS. Go over the stile and then the one immediately to its L. Follow the fence and then the wall and, after crossing one more stile, reach a farm road ½ mile (800 m) beyond the Sugarloaf. Turn immediately L through the gate and, heading for Summerhill Farm, follow the R wall up to the next gate. Cross the field diagonally, passing an old lime kiln on the L, and go through a passage between walls into the next field. Cross this, again diagonally, to a similar passage, and turn half L to follow the wall through a gap and over a stile to turn R on a clear path a few yards down the hillside. In the valley below is Swainsley Hall, built in 1867 by a London solicitor, with a dovecote in its grounds. The Manifold Railway ran through a tunnel behind the hall, to conceal it from the owners.

The path stays level and then sweeps round the great bowl-shaped hillside above the Ecton Copper Mines (1), gradually dropping to the spoil heaps of the Dutchman Mine. Ahead is the engine house of Deep Ecton Mine and here the path doubles back along the ridge beside the wall, passing fenced, open mineshafts to a stile. The path continues on the L-hand side of the ridge, passing more shafts and levels, through two wall gaps and over three stiles to the ruined buildings of Waterbank Mine.

From the mine, the road is reached after 300 yards (270 m) at a gate. Turn L down the road and, ignoring the L turning, continue through the gate and down the road for ½ mile (800 m) to Pepper Inn, now a private house, but once used as an isolation hospital when there was an outbreak of smallpox among navvies building the Manifold Light Railway.

Wetton Mill on the River Manifold

A stile opposite leads to a small bridge over the stream, and then a wall on the R is followed up to a stile in the corner over the fence. Cross the field half L to the next stile and straight ahead over the brow of the hill to a stile with a quarry on the R. Crossing the stile ahead, go through the gate opposite and down the farm lane to the village of Wetton. Turn R and walk through the village to the far end. Turn R at the T-junction and then L at the fork (sign 'Concession Footpath'). In just under ½ mile (800 m) go through a gate and over the stile to the R (PFS). Go L down to the gap in the ruined wall at the corner, across the dip and up to a stile. A short steep climb leads to the summit of the cliffs above Thor's Cave. Be very careful; the cliff edge is unprotected and quite sheer.

Return the same way and turn L to circle down to the base of the cliffs at the entrance to Thor's Cave *(2)*. Once this huge natural cavern has been explored, a flight of stone steps will lead you down to the River Manifold. The river is usually dry, but is crossed by a substantial bridge. Turn R on the old track of the Manifold Light Railway *(3)* and in ½ mile (800 m), crossing another bridge, turn L to follow either of two parallel roads back to the car-park at Wetton Mill *(4)*.

1 Ecton Copper Mines

In the eighteenth century, Deep Ecton Mine was a very profitable mine for its owner the Duke of Devonshire, with

43

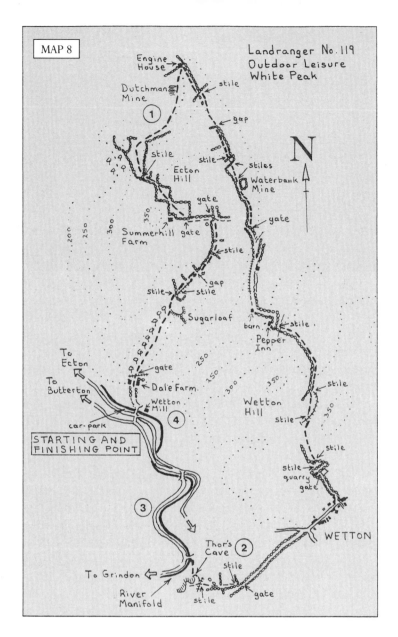

MAP 8

Engine House

Dutchman Mine

stile

gap

1

stile

stile

stiles

Ecton Hill

Waterbank Mine

gate

gate

Summerhill gate

Farm

stile

gap

stile → ← stile

Sugarloaf

barn

stile

Pepper Inn

To Ecton

gate

To Butterton

Dale Farm

Wetton Mill

Wetton Hill

stile

stile

car-park

4

STARTING AND FINISHING POINT

stile

stile

quarry gate

3

WETTON

Thor's Cave 2

stile

To Grindon

stile

gate

River Manifold

stile

Landranger No.119
Outdoor Leisure
White Peak

N

profits amounting to over one million pounds. It was, at 1380 ft (420 m), the deepest mine in Great Britain.

Deep Ecton Mine was just one of a number of copper mines to be found at Ecton, all of which are now disused and in ruins. The Ecton copper mines also saw in 1670 the earliest use in Britain of gunpowder in mining and at its peak around 300 men, women and children worked here. Sixty men worked a six-hour shift for about 5p, while boys removed the ore to be crushed above ground by women and girls. Although the Ecton copper mines did not suffer the serious water problems often found elsewhere in the Peak, a 32 ft

Opposite *Near
Alstonefield*

44

diameter (10 m) waterwheel was built underground to power drainage pumps and boats were used as transport some 200 ft (60 m) beneath the River Manifold. The engine house, still in use as a barn, held a Boulton and Watt engine which raised waste rock to the surface, forming great spoil heaps since removed for road making. The mines finally ceased production in the late nineteenth century.

Thor's Cave

Thor's Cave, the cave of the Norse Thunder God, looks down on the Manifold Valley from a very large main entrance, 30 ft (9 m) high and over 20 ft (6 m) wide. A second side entrance, West Window, faces down the valley. First excavated by Samuel Carrington from Wetton in 1864, the cave has yielded stone querns, pottery fragments, bronze brooches, iron knives and bones from Romano-British times. Much has probably been lost by the early excavators who made a large spoil heap outside the cave entrance. The pieces of tape seen hanging from high in the roof are left by rock climbers whose spectacular climb 'Thor' goes up the wall, crosses the roof and then ascends the cliff.

Manifold Light Railway

Opened in 1904 and closed again by 1934, this railway fell between the heyday of steam and the modern preservation societies who would surely have rescued it. It took two years to build and was said by a navvy to 'start from nowhere and end up in the same place'. A private, narrow gauge railway of 2 ft 6 in (762 mm), it operated mainly as a milk train, supplementing meagre passenger traffic with excursion trains at weekends and public holidays. There was a connecting milk train from the main line at Waterhouses from 1919 and 300 churns a day were carried. When the dairy closed in 1933 the railway rapidly succumbed, being converted to a footpath in 1937.

Wetton Mill

Wetton Mill, now a farm, but originally a corn mill, was first mentioned in records of 1577. The bridge is much later, dating from 1807. Just above the bridge at Wetton Mill is a limestone hummock, full of interesting holes, known as Nan Tor Cave. The River Manifold disappears just below the mill and travels 5 miles (8 km) underground before reappearing at the 'Boil Hole' in the grounds of Ilam Hall. Sir Thomas Wardle of Swainsley Hall unsuccessfully attempted to block the swallow holes with concrete, but the river won and only sometimes, usually in winter, appears above ground.

2·9

WELLINGTON'S AND NELSON'S MONUMENTS

This visit to the matching monuments to Nelson and Wellington, which face each other across the valley, contrasts the
grandeur of the rugged and wild edges with the formality of
Chatsworth Estate.

ROUTE DESCRIPTION (Maps 9, 10)

Turn R out of the car-park where there is a prominent
guidestone which marked the junction of several old packhorse
routes, and in a few yards turn L at a stile by the sign 'Boundary
of Open Country'. Notice also the important admonition nailed
to the tree 'No manure removal', so be sure to clean your boots!
Either follow the wide track which leads to the Eagle Stone, or
the edge of the escarpment where the view is better. Passing the
Eagle Stone *(1)*, reach the edge and turn L to arrive at
Wellington's Monument *(2)*.

Walk east from Wellington's Monument along the broad
footpath on the edge of the moor, which is fringed with silver
birch and rowan. Shortly before the main road there is another
guidestone on the R which is inscribed 'CHESTE RFEILD
ROADE' ('Road to Chesterfield'). Unusually it is marked on one
face only. On reaching the road at a gate, turn R downhill to the
crossroads. Crossing over the A621, take the ladder stile at the
boundary to open country. Bear almost immediately L off the
major track and follow the track heading directly for Birchen
Edge. The ground to the left of this track is out of bounds. After
scattered birch trees and some boggy ground, a short steep
climb on a narrow path to the L leads to the top of the edge
close to the OS trig point.

The crag reaches its highest point at Nelson's Monument *(3)*,
a less imposing memorial than Wellington's and often treated
with scant respect by climbers who use it as a belay. Follow the
path along the edge and, at the Water Board manhole covers,
the path turns R and descends the edge. Upon reaching the
broad path at its foot, turn L with a golf course on your R. At

STARTING AND
FINISHING POINT
Curbar Gap
National Park car-
park east of Curbar
(119-261748).

LENGTH
6½ miles (10.5 km)

ASCENT
850 ft (260 m)

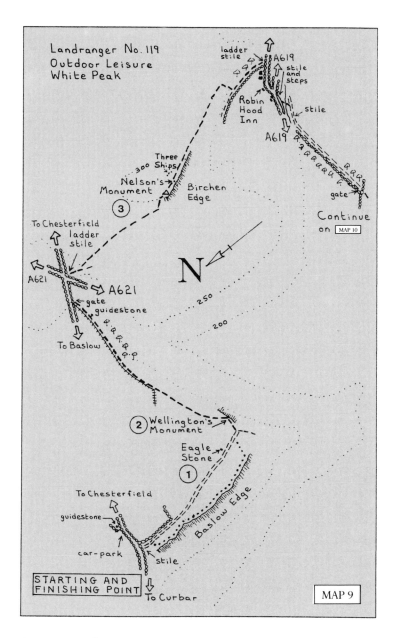

the main road climb a ladder stile over the wall and turn R down the road to join the A619 at the Robin Hood Inn.

Shortly after the Eric Byne campsite entrance, cross the A619 and take the path at the wooden sign 'Concessionary Footpath to Baslow'. A steep flight of steps leads down to a stout wooden bridge. Joining a broad track, turn R and follow the yellow waymarks of the concessionary footpath over a stile and along the lane for ½ mile (800 m) to a gate into a field. At the next stile Chatsworth Park is entered and in 300 yards (270 m) Jubilee Rock (4) will be found a few paces off the track to the L. Follow the indistinct path across the open parkland, marked

Opposite
Curbar from
Baslow Edge

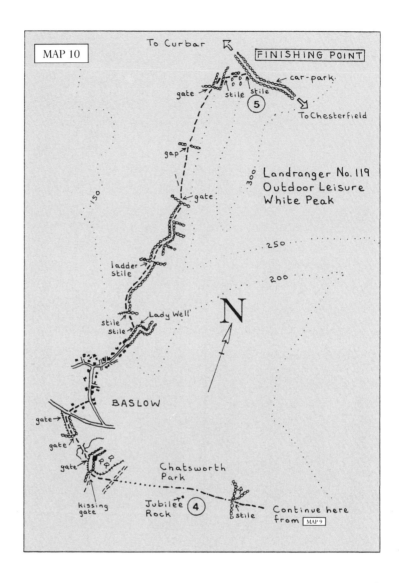

occasionally with yellow waymarks, to leave Chatsworth Park at 'The Kissing Gate'.

In 50 yards (45 m) turn L through a small kissing gate into the field and then across the hump-backed bridge. Cross the next field to a gate. Go along a path flanked by a stone wall and fence to a flight of steps which will bring you into Baslow at a gate just before the road. Cross the road and go up the narrow path opposite, just to the Ŕ of 'Ashton Fields' house. Turn L onto the next road. At Barr road turn R and, where the metalled surface deteriorates to a track just before Lady Well, turn L through a stile. Follow a rising grassy path to a stile and through the fields to the L of a wall to a ladder stile.

Joining a more major track, follow this between gritstone walls to emerge again onto open country at a gate below Baslow Edge. At the Y-fork take the R branch and continue at the same level on a sandy path through the bracken. At the open country sign, go through a gate onto a wide, green lane which rises to meet the road near Curbar Gap. Turn R at the National Trust sign and through a squeezer stile to avoid the road walking. Emerging onto the road at a stile, a gritstone slab on the R is inscribed with a Biblical text *(5)*. The car-park is a few yards up the road.

Climbers on Curbar Edge

1 *Eagle Stone*

Many years ago the young men of Baslow were required to demonstrate their fitness for the responsibilities of marriage by ascending this rock. Nowadays it is the rocks of the edge itself which attract climbers, and anyway, as the climber Morley Wood once said of the climb 'Bachelor's Buttress' at the Roaches, 'Married men are more used to taking risks than bachelors'. These crags are sometimes used by the mountain rescue teams for practising lowering stretchers down the rockface. The quarry on the edge at this point was in use as late as the 1930s.

2 *Wellington's Monument*

The monument is inscribed 'Wellington Born 1769 Died 1852. Erected 1866 by E.M. Wrench late 34th Reg'mt'. From here there is a good view across the valley to Gardom's Edge and also to Nelson's Monument.

3 *Nelson's Monument*

This monument was erected in 1810 by John Brightman, a Baslow man, predating Wellington's Monument by some fifty years. The date 1865 inscribed on the obelisk appears to point to graffiti not being a modern phenomenon. There are three rocks nearby commemorating the ships of Nelson's fleet, *Victory*, *Defiant* and *Royal Soverin*.

4 *Jubilee Rock*

Chatsworth Park was the creation of the fourth Duke of Devonshire, 1720–1764, who employed the landscape architect Lancelot (Capability) Brown. The shape of the woods which follow the contour of the hills is typical of Brown's work. Situated in the park, the Jubilee Rock, carved to commemorate Queen Victoria's golden jubilee, reads:

1837

SEND HER	V	HAPPY
VICTORIOUS	I	AND GLORIOUS
	T Ⓒ R	
LONG TO	I	GOD
REIGN OVER US	A	SAVE THE QUEEN

1887

5 *Biblical Text*

This slab is inscribed 'Hebrews 7 25' and is one of several such slabs in the vicinity which were carved by Edwin Gregory, a mole-catcher and local preacher.

2·10

RINGING ROGER AND GRINDSLOW KNOLL

This popular walk from Edale encircles the Grindsbrook Valley keeping close to the edge of the Kinder plateau. There is the feel of the mountains about this walk with the steep drop into the valley always at your side. After a strenuous ascent, Ringing Roger is reached, and, from the summit rocks round to Grindslow Knoll, walkers can be seen far below on their way up Grindsbrook Clough at the start of their long journey north on the Pennine Way.

STARTING AND
FINISHING POINT
Edale car-park
(110-124853).

LENGTH
6 miles (9 km)

ASCENT
1200 ft (375 m)

ROUTE DESCRIPTION (Map 11)

From the car-park turn R under the railway bridge and up into Edale village *(1)* to the Old Nag's Head. Follow the signs for the Pennine Way *(2)* up the unsurfaced track to the iron gates. A PWS points R on a path which leads down some steps to a

Nether Tor

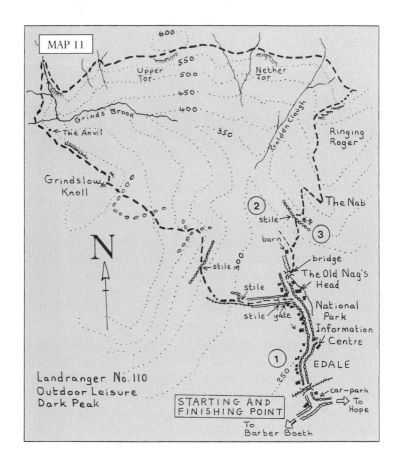

bridge. Go along the footpath a short way to a small barn and then turn R and follow the clear path up the field to a stile by Fred Heardman's Plantation *(3)*. The path zig-zags up the hillside to The Nab, which is a good viewpoint for the Vale of Edale spread out below. Contour round towards Golden Clough until you reach the spot immediately below Ringing Roger, and then strike up the hillside directly to the rocks. From the summit, head towards an area of bare rock and sand, and then turn L onto the path which keeps to the edge of the plateau. Crossing Golden Clough, the rocks of Nether Tor on the L are where the stone for Edale Church was quarried.

The path continues along the edge passing the highest point at Upper Tor where Pym Chair can be seen on the distant skyline to the west. Continue to the head of Grindsbrook Clough where it is necessary to turn R and detour for 200 yards (180 m) to avoid the great ravine. Double back on the far side and follow the path round towards Grindslow Knoll, passing the Anvil Stone. The summit of Grindslow Knoll, in just over ¼

Opposite
Golden Clough

54

mile (400 m), can be missed as the path does not cross the highest point which is a few yards off to the R.

Descend now south-east towards Edale far below. Soon the eroded path improves to a track which leads down to a stile and fields beyond. Cross the field towards a fence and then cross a wall at a stile. A sunken path between hedges is joined, which soon arrives at a stile and a kissing gate opposite the Old Nag's Head. Turn R and walk back down the road to the car-park.

1 *Edale Village*

The village of Edale, the island valley, has two pubs, both of which at one time came under the jurisdiction of Fred Heardman (see *(3)*). There is also a café, an excellent Peak Park Information Centre and several campsites. Despite Edale's popularity, it has not been spoilt and manages to retain much of its charm. Five packhorse ways converged here and there is a good example of a narrow packhorse bridge crossing Grinds Brook only yards from the Old Nag's Head.

2 *The Pennine Way*

Britain's first and most celebrated long-distance footpath stretches 250 miles (400 km) from Edale in the south to Kirk Yetholm over the border in Scotland. This high level route, which follows the Pennine backbone of England, was conceived by Tom Stephenson in 1935; but it took thirty years of dedicated and persistent negotiation before it was finally opened on 24 April 1965. As many as 10 000 people a year start on the route, and, although not all of these complete the walk (it is a tough undertaking), its popularity has led to erosion problems such as the four-lane highway up Grindsbrook Clough.

3 *Fred Heardman's Plantation*

This plantation is dedicated to the memory of Fred Heardman, a legendary figure of the Peak District who was, for many years, the landlord of both the Old Nag's Head and the Church Inn (now the Rambler Inn). Known to his friends as Bill the Bogtrotter for his exploits on arduous walks and runs in the Peak, he became a rural district councillor and fought, fortunately very successfully, against the industrialization of this attractive valley. He was also a member of the Peak District Branch of the Council for the Preservation of Rural England, and when the Peak District National Park was formed, the Nag's Head became their first information centre and mountain rescue post.

Opposite
Ringing Roger

MONSAL DALE AND ASHFORD IN THE WATER

STARTING AND
FINISHING POINT
White Lodge car-
park (119-170705).
On the A6 Buxton–
Bakewell road,
3 miles (5 km) west
of Bakewell.

LENGTH
8½ miles (13.5 km)

ASCENT
800 ft (240 m)

The lower reaches of the River Wye pass through Monsal Dale, spanned by the great viaduct of the old Buxton to Derby railway, and on down past the village of Ashford in the Water, which is famed for its well dressing, to the town of Bakewell.

Packhorse bridges and old mills blend into the scene, complementing the natural beauty of the dale; while the railway itself becomes in summer a wild flower garden which links with the Wye to form a varied and interesting walk.

ROUTE DESCRIPTION (Maps 12–14)

Cross the A6 to a stile in the wall opposite. Descend to a small stream and over a wooden ladder stile, where in summer the banks of the stream are covered in the bright yellow flowers of musk. Through the woodland beyond (PFS 'Monsal Dale') the first view of the River Wye is seen. On the opposite bank is Fin Cop, whose top is the site of an Iron Age hill fort.

Follow the river upstream for 1¼ miles (2 km) to a stile and under Monsal Viaduct (1). At the footbridge over the river, turn half L through the stile (PFS 'Brushfield and Taddington Dale') and ascend to the disused railway. Go over the stile (sign 'Monsal Trail') to join the railway where the blocked up entrance of a lead mine can be seen opposite. Turn L towards the tunnel to emerge suddenly on the very exposed heights of Monsal Viaduct. Just before the tunnel turn L and after 100 yards (90 m) turn R onto another track. Continue to climb until a flight of stone steps brings you out, somewhat breathless, to Monsal Head (café, pub and toilets).

Cross the B6465 and take the road opposite (an old turnpike) to Little Longstone. Passing the Congregational Church, enter the village and go past (or through!) the Packhorse Inn to turn R over a stone step stile (PFS 'Ashford 1½ ml) just past the last house on the R. Bear half R across four fields to rejoin the tracks of the disused railway. Turn L on the railway and in ¼ mile (400 m) pass through the old station at Thornbridge Hall. Soon

Opposite *Sheepwash
Bridge, Ashford in the
Water*

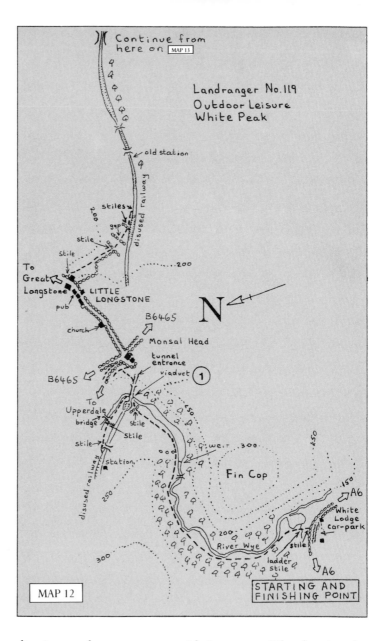

Continue from here on MAP 13

Landranger No.119
Outdoor Leisure
White Peak

old station

stiles

gap

stile

stile

200

To
Great
Longstone

LITTLE
LONGSTONE

disused railway

pub

B6465

church

Monsal Head

tunnel
entrance

viaduct ①

B6465

To
Upperdale
bridge

stile

stile

stile

weir   .300.

station

250

Fin Cop

disused railway

250

150

A6

White
Lodge
Car-park

200

River Wye

stile

300

ladder
stile

A6

MAP 12

STARTING AND
FINISHING POINT

the view to the L opens out with Longstone Edge forming the skyline in the distance. One mile (1.6 km) beyond the station, opposite the Rowdale toll-bar house, with the bell and gate symbol on its gable, take the footpath turning R through a wooden gate (PFS 'Bakewell'). Follow the green path, enclosed by stone walls, over the hill through seven gates to a track to the road.

Go straight ahead to cross Holme Bridge *(2)* and then R onto the A6. Just after the factory, turn R through a stile. Cross the field and go through a narrow path between the houses crossing a road to emerge again into open fields. Follow the meadows to

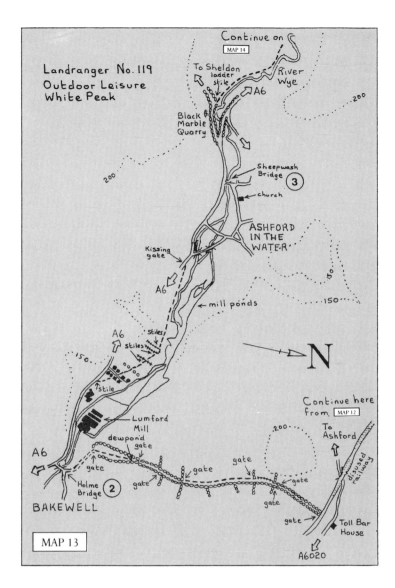

Continue on
MAP 14

Landranger No. 119
Outdoor Leisure
White Peak

To Sheldon
ladder
stile

River
Wye

A6

200

Black
Marble
Quarry

Sheepwash
Bridge (3)

← church

ASHFORD
IN THE
WATER

Kissing
gate

A6

← mill ponds

150

A6   stiles
stiles

150

stile

N

Continue here
from MAP 12

Lumford
Mill

200

To
Ashford

dewpond
gate

A6

gate

gate

gate

gate

Holme (2)
Bridge

gate

gate

disused railway

BAKEWELL

gate

gate

Toll Bar
House

MAP 13

A6020

Ashford, over three stiles and passing the millponds, to emerge
onto the A6 at a kissing gate. Turn R to cross the two bridges.
Over the road, enter Ashford in the Water *(3)* and turn L by the
village store to pass the Church of the Holy Trinity. At the end
where the street turns R, Sheepwash Bridge will be seen on the
L. Turn L over the bridge to the A6. Cross this and turn R to gain
the footpath on the far side. After about 300 yards (260 m) take
the minor road (PFS 'Monsal Dale avoiding A6 road'), passing on
the L the Ashford Black Marble Quarry (worked until 1905).
Two hundred yards (180 m) along this road, just past a bridge
on the site of the Black Marble Mill, turn R (PFS 'Monsal Dale
via White Lodge') and over a ladder stile.
   Follow the fields beside the river for ½ mile (800 m) to a stile
and the remains of old mills, one of which used to pump

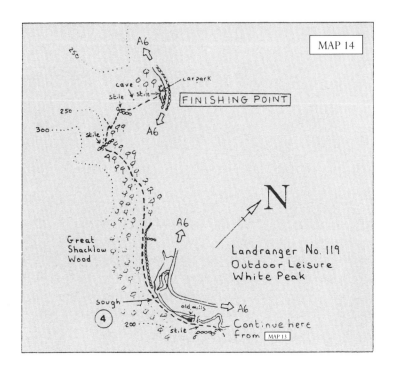

MAP 14

drinking water up to Sheldon. Go behind the mills into Great Shacklow Wood and in 200 yards (180 m) the sough of Magpie Mine *(4)* will be seen entering the river on the R. The path now climbs up the hillside and in ⅔ mile (1.1 km) descends to a stile. Continue to the lowest point of the path and turn R (PBS 'Bridleway to A6'). Cross the stile, turn R, and shortly before arriving back at the car-park there is, hidden in the trees above, Taddington Dale Resurgence Cave from which a stream issues in wet weather.

1 Monsal Viaduct

Monsal Viaduct is a most spectacular feature. Built in 1867, the Midland railway ran here until it was closed in 1968, and now the viaduct has been declared of architectural and historic interest. John Ruskin, the nineteenth-century English author and art critic, was less enthusiastic about the railway, declaring 'You enterprised a railroad through the valley – you blasted its rocks away, heaped thousands of tons of shale into its lovely stream. The valley is gone and the Gods with it, and now every fool in Buxton can be at Bakewell in half an hour and every fool in Bakewell at Buxton; which you think a lucrative process of exchange – you Fools everywhere.'

If the weather is unkind it is worth knowing that by turning R instead of L on joining the railway, one of the old buildings of the Monsal Dale railway station will be found still standing.

Opposite Monsal
Dale *from Monsal
Head*

62

2 *Holme Bridge*

This was rebuilt in 1664 on a packhorse route to the north. The bridge was probably built at this point in order to avoid payment of tolls at Bakewell itself. A corn mill at Bakewell, recorded as far back as the *Domesday Book*, was supplied with water from this river. When, in 1778, Lumford Mill was built by Richard Arkwright and a reservoir was constructed for the new mill, a bypass leat was built to feed the old mill; this however was not entirely adequate for the purpose, to the annoyance of its owner the Duke of Rutland. In 1852, with the addition of two larger waterwheels to Lumford Mill, another reservoir was constructed upstream, as well as a new channel; while a weir was built in the river to improve the supply to the corn mill.

3 *Ashford in the Water*

Ashford in the Water is one of the villages which continues the ancient tradition of well dressing. About 150 years ago the present floral patterns were introduced. Petals, berries, bark and suchlike are pressed into a bed of clay to form beautiful pictures and patterns. As many as five wells are dressed in Ashford for Trinity Sunday and can be seen for the following week.

Sheepwash Bridge is a medieval packhorse bridge; 'sheep-wash' refers to the practice of washing sheep by driving them into the river and making them swim across to emerge on the other side.

The name Ashford comes from the Saxon 'Aescforda', where the Old Portway forded the river, and is mentioned in the *Domesday Book* with a reference to 'plumbariae' or places where lead was smelted.

4 *Magpie Mine Sough*

The sough, or drainage tunnel, drains the Magpie Mine. The scree above the entrance indicates the site of the massive explosion which tore this hillside apart and partially blocked the river on 23 April 1966. Water had built up behind a blockage in the mine and eventually burst forth, fortunately without injuring anyone. The Magpie Mine was being worked for lead as early as 1795 and probably earlier than that. The Peak District Mines Historical Society use the main buildings at Sheldon as a Field Centre. The Magpie sough, driven in 1873, and large enough to be navigable by boat, was probably one of the last major soughs dug in this area.

2·12

ABNEY MOOR AND BRETTON CLOUGH

Abney Moor, an isolated piece of moorland cut off from the larger and wilder northern moors by Hope Valley, is a quiet and peaceful place where the gliders from Great Hucklow soar in the sky above. The beauties of Bretton Clough will also be appreciated by connoisseurs of the Peak District, with its pleasant tree-lined streams in little steep-sided valleys.

Eyam Edge, the starting point, is an excellent viewpoint. Northwards is Stanage Edge, and through a gap in the intervening hills Win Hill and Derwent Edge can be seen.

STARTING AND FINISHING POINT
Great Hucklow to Eyam road (119-190781).

LENGTH
8½ miles (13.5 km)

ASCENT
800 ft (240 m)

ROUTE DESCRIPTION (Maps 15-17)

Cross the stile and descend the very steep field beside the wall. On the R is an interesting series of hummocks and hills which are the result of landslips. Bretton Brook ('Bretton' meaning 'farm of the Britons') at the foot of the slope is crossed by a footbridge and the track followed uphill to a stile on the L. Continue straight ahead, keeping near the wall, to the next stile on the R; and then head L of the farm to cross a stile onto the farm track. Turn L towards the road and then R to a stile (PFS 'Bradwell') which gives access to Abney Moor.

Follow the clear path across Abney Moor for 1 mile (1.6 km). On many days gliders from the Great Hucklow Gliding Club (1) circle high in the sky above the moor. Leave the moor over a stile onto the old packhorse way from Bradwell to Eyam. Turn R and follow it for about ¾ mile (1.2 km), past the end of the road down to Abney (PBS) until the wall turns R. Turn L (PBS), and in 100 yards (90 m) go through gateposts on to the walled Shatton Lane. Straight ahead, the Great Ridge of Mam Tor to Lose Hill can be seen across the valley. Follow the old lane for 1 mile (1.6 km) with Shatton Edge on the R, first through a gate and then past a tall TV repeater mast, until the lane turns L just after another gate. A ladder stile at the corner leads back to the moor and in a few yards a wall comes in from the L. Follow this wall for about a mile (1.6 km) until the road is met near Offerton

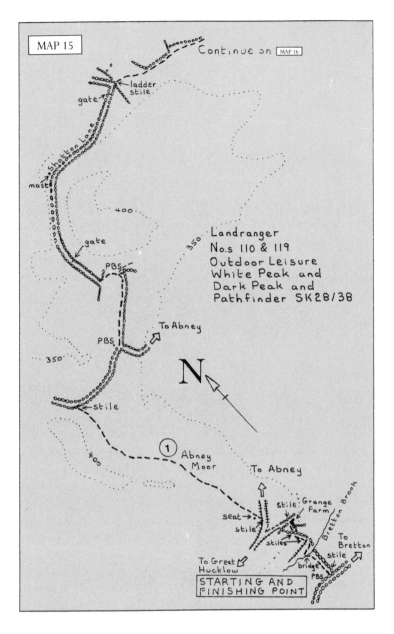

Continue on MAP 16

Hall at a stile. Turn R onto this and walk uphill. In ¼ mile (400 m) a stile on the L leads to an attractive footpath which is followed down to a stile just before Callow Farm. At the farm, turn L and through a small gate. Go downhill, crossing a broken wall, and enter the wood at another small gate below the farm.

Go through the wood and out into a field at a stile. Cross the field and turn R out of the gate onto the lane, which after about ¼ mile (400 m) passes the entrance to a house and leads up to the road. Go straight across the road, over a stile and half L up the field to another stile on the top of the ridge. Now go R and downhill where a line of signposts leads to the farm road. The

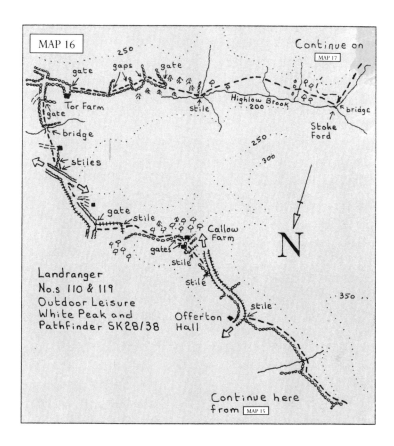

MAP 16

Continue on
MAP 17

Continue here
from MAP 15

Tor Farm

gate gaps gate

stile

Highlow Brook
200

bridge

Stoke
Ford

bridge

stiles

gate

stile

Callow
Farm

gates

stile

Landranger
No.s 110 & 119
Outdoor Leisure
White Peak and
Pathfinder SK28/38

stile

stile

Offerton
Hall

N

bridge immediately below and the stile on its far side lead to a field whose L-hand wall should be followed up to a gate and lane. At the top of the lane turn R and go down towards Tor Farm, passing through a gate on the L just before the farm. Beside the wall a path leads through three field gateways and then a gate into woodland. After passing over a stile in the wood and a stream, the track climbs steadily up the hill through oak and silver birch onto the moorland. In ½ mile (800 m), and having crossed a small clough, Stoke Ford is reached, which is the meeting of several old tracks and has a bridge across the main stream.

Turn L at Stoke Ford (not across the bridge) and climb uphill. In a few yards the track forks. Take the R fork which follows Bretton Brook. In ¼ mile (400 m) you come to a stile and then a little, steep-sided clough. Climbing out of the clough past a ruined barn, go through four ruined walls and into woodland where on meeting a fence turn L to follow it down to a stile and stream. Zig-zag up the hillside and over a stile into fields. Follow the R-hand wall to another stile onto a farm lane. In ¼ mile (400 m) the lane comes out at the Barrel Inn. Turn R and ¾ mile (1.2 km) down the road is the starting point.

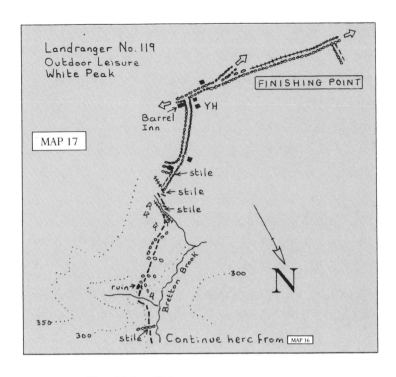

Landranger No. 119
Outdoor Leisure
White Peak

FINISHING POINT

YH

Barrel
Inn

MAP 17

stile

stile

stile

Bretton Brook

·300

N

ruin→

350····

300

stile

Continue here from MAP 16

1 Great Hucklow Gliding Club

The club, officially known as the Derbyshire and Lancashire Gliding Club, was formed in 1935 by a group of local flyers, who leased Camp Hill, and the Manchester Aeronautical Society, who flew from the Barrel Inn in 1934. The remains of an Ancient Briton fort on the south and south-west edge of Camp Hill also cut across the field to the inconvenience of the club. The field itself is private property.

There was a break in flying during World War II when the club was banned from using the airfield and obstructions were placed on the field, but now it has 165 flying members and on a busy day there can be as many as thirty gliders in the air at once. The gliders are towed by winch to a height of 1000–1100 ft (305–335 m) before being released. A winch is used because powered aircraft are not allowed by the Peak District Park Authorities, and also the conditions are very windy and are not really suitable for them. The club owns three single-seater and three dual-seater planes. Many of the members have their own aircraft and often these are syndicated, each owner having a quarter share. Members come mostly from Sheffield, Nottingham and South Manchester, although one comes all the way from Glasgow.

The club height record is 23 000 ft (7 000 m), and the distance record stands at 317 miles (510 km).

Eyam Woodlands

2·13

THE GREAT RIDGE FROM CASTLETON

STARTING AND
FINISHING POINT
Car-park
(110-139827)
opposite Speedwell
Cavern at the foot
of Winnats Pass
near Castleton.

LENGTH
8 miles (13 km)

ASCENT
1500 ft (460 m)

The Great Ridge stretches for just two miles from Mam Tor to Lose Hill, giving an aerial view of the vale of Edale on one side and of Hope Valley and Castleton on the other. The walk starts by climbing Winnats Pass, an impressive limestone gorge, and returns beside Peakshole Water, past its source in Castleton where it issues from Peak Cavern, one of several interesting show caves in the village.

ROUTE DESCRIPTION (Maps 18, 19)

From the car-park walk up Winnats Pass (1) with the cliffs towering above on either side. At the top of the pass turn R over a stile (PFS). Follow the wall beside the farm and over two stiles to the road. Go straight over the stile opposite and past Windy Knoll Cave on the L, where the bones of Ice Age mammoths were found, to a stile onto the A625. Crossing this, climb up the hillside to a stile onto the road at Mam Nick. Turn immediately R over a stile where a flight of steps, provided by the National Trust to repair the eroded path, is joined leading to the summit of Mam Tor and the Great Ridge (2). At the top of the steps there is a good view of the ramparts of an Iron Age hill fort. Descending from the summit, the remains of the A625 can be seen down on the R. After passing a gate, Hollins Cross is the next low point on the ridge, where an old packhorse route from Castleton to Edale is crossed. Going over two stiles to top the next rise, Back Tor is seen ahead with its almost sheer north-east face. Cross the stile in the dip and climb very steeply up the slope to the top of Back Tor. Lose Hill, the last summit on the Great Ridge, is ½ mile (800 m) further on.

Go over Lose Hill summit. As the path begins to descend, it turns R and goes down the slopes to a double stile. Follow the broad ridge down to a fence and stile. Then at the next stile by a barn, a sunken track is joined, and this leads down to a stile and the lane at Townhead. Turn L and in 300 yards (270 m) join the road to Hope where you turn R, and after ¾ mile (1.2 km) the

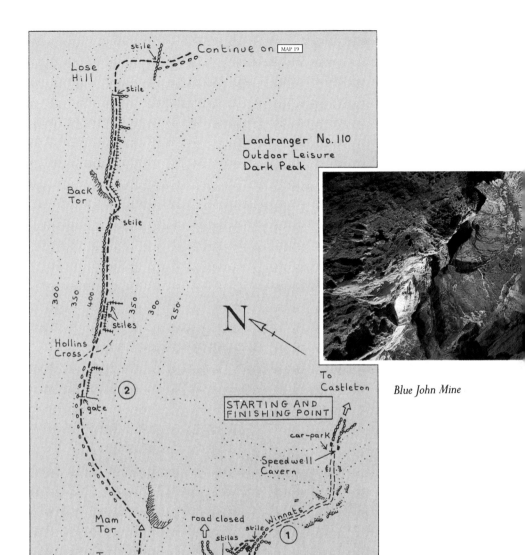

Blue John Mine

village of Hope is reached. Going R onto the A625 and then immediately L by the church, take the next R fork (sign 'Pindale'). In a few yards turn R over a stile and follow the river-bank. One stile is met before the single track railway which serves the Hope Cement Works *(3)* is crossed. Take care to watch for any trains. Peakshole Water now veers away from the path which is followed over the fields, crossing three more stiles, until it mets a lane which leads back to the main road.

Turn L onto the road and walk up into Castleton *(4)*. Follow the main road round the S-bend into the main street and then turn L up Castle Street past the National Park Information

71

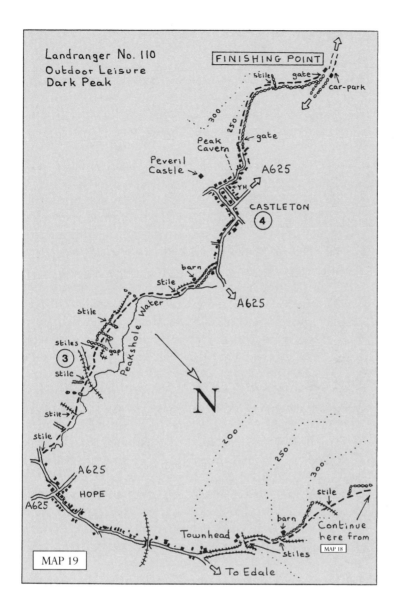

Continue here from MAP 18

MAP 19

Centre. Peveril Castle is seen ahead on the skyline, with the entrance below at the end of the street. It is open all year round. Turn R by the Youth Hostel (sign 'Peak Cavern') and follow the road down to cross Peakshole Water. The footpath on the L leads up to Peak Cavern. Continue along the road, which shortly becomes a track, and go through the gate into the fields. The wall is now followed for ½ mile (800 m), crossing a stile, to arrive at a gate opposite the car-park.

1 Winnats Pass

This narrow road, with a gradient of 1 in 5, climbs between towering limestone cliffs which are best seen on foot rather than from a car. This old packhorse way and saltway,

Opposite *The Great Ridge from Lose Hill*

turnpiked in 1758, was a major highway until the construction in 1817 of a new road round the foot of Mam Tor. However, recent years has seen much more traffic in the pass since the losing battle with landslips led to the closure of the A625 in 1979.

In 1758 a young eloping couple were robbed and murdered in the pass and their bodies thrown into the Speedwell Mine. The saddle of their horse is in the small museum at the Speedwell Mine. Speedwell Mine is open to the public and visitors are taken by boat along an underground canal to the 'Bottomless Pit'.

2 *The Great Ridge*

Mam Tor ('the mother rock') is composed of alternate layers of sandstone and shale, exposed in the great precipice. This is a highly unstable combination which has given rise to Mam Tor's other name, the Shivering Mountain. The summit is ringed by the massive ramparts of an Iron Age fort, cut into by the continually slipping cliff. A packhorse track skirts the north face of Mam Tor, and then follows the ridge to Hollins Cross and down to Hope on the southern slopes of Lose Hill. Until 1633, when a chapel was built at Edale, funeral processions had to climb over the ridge for burial at Hope. Edale Mill, a corn mill, tannery and then a cotton mill, was powered by the River Noe. When it was enlarged in 1795, about 100 women were employed, many of them walking over each day via Hollins Cross from Castleton. The mill closed in 1934 and is now converted into flats.

3 *Hope Cement Works*

Limestone and shale are the essential components of cement and Hope Cement Works, constructed in 1933, is strategically placed at the geological junction of the two. A branch line joins the works to the main railway line over concrete bridges which are quite out of character with the area. The quarry is gradually devouring the limestone to the south and, although providing much needed local employment, limestone quarries and a National Park make uncomfortable companions.

4 *Castleton*

First recorded in 1196, this is essentially a medieval new town. Unlike most mining towns, it was planned, rather than being built by random extensions. Set out under the castle, it ceased to prosper when the castle lost its importance in the fourteenth century. The castle, which was built by William Peveril, William the Conqueror's local bailiff, dates from the

eleventh century. The rectangular keep is late Norman of about 1175. A dry ditch isolates the castle yard, which occupies nearly the whole of the summit, from the rest of the hill. By the seventeenth century the castle was in ruins.

Looking towards Castleton from Hollins Cross

Castleton is famed for its show caves; Speedwell Mine at the foot of Winnats Pass, Treak Cliff Cavern, Blue John Mine, and Peak Cavern, whose entrance, 40 ft (12 m) high and 100 ft (30 m) wide, was once used for rope making. Blue John, which is a blue and yellow coloured fluorspar, is used in the manufacture of ornaments and jewelry which are sold in the local shops.

KINDER SCOUT FROM HAYFIELD

STARTING AND
FINISHING POINT
Car-park on Kinder
Road, Hayfield
(110-049869).

LENGTH
8 miles (13 km)

ASCENT
1400 ft (430 m)

This is one of the most popular walks from Hayfield. The navigation is relatively easy as the walk sticks mainly to the edge of the Kinder plateau, but it gives the flavour of the wild moorland summit. The highlight of the walk is Kinder Downfall. In hard winters this can freeze to a magnificent wall of ice; while if there is much water in the river and a westerly wind is blowing, the water fails to fall at all and instead is ·blown upwards, arching back over the edge.

ROUTE DESCRIPTION (Maps 20, 21)

Turn L out of the quarry car-park, where there is a plaque to the Kinder Trespass *(1)*, and walk up Kinder Road for nearly ½ mile (400 m) to the gates of the Water Treatment Works. Turn R over the bridge, follow the farm road for about 50 yards (45 m), then go L (PFS 'KINDER 1') and through a small gate to follow the stream up to the next bridge. Cross this, past the mountain rescue post sign, and go through the small gate opposite. Go up the steep path and follow the wall beside Kinder Reservoir to William Clough.

The path up William Clough *(2)* crosses and recrosses the stream innumerable times. Climb up until you reach the watershed at the top. In front is the start of Ashop Clough which descends to the Snake Road. The three-fingered signpost (PWS) points all ways except the one you should go, which is R and up the steep slopes onto the Kinder Scout plateau. At the top of the steep ascent, turn half R and follow the edge of the plateau. In just under a mile (1.6 km), where the rocks form a cliff, there is a white-painted cross on the rocks nearest the edge, embellished with symbols and the initials G K. This is the sacred spot of the Etherios Society whose leader is George King. Continue along the edge for ½ mile (800 m) to reach Kinder Downfall. If it is in spate you may have to make quite a detour to avoid getting a soaking from the blown back spray.

Crossing the River Kinder, continue along the edge now in a

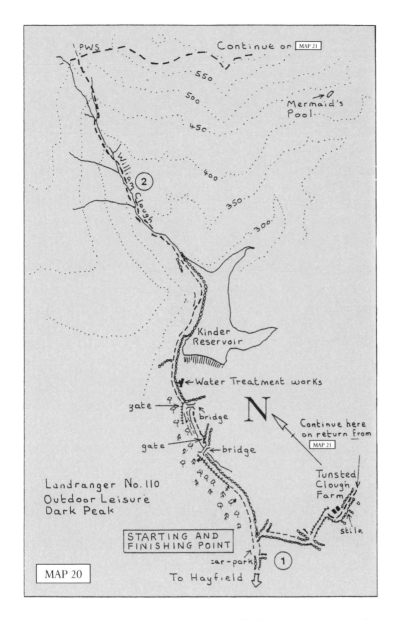

PWS — — — — · · · · · Continue on [MAP 21]

550

500

Mermaid's Pool →0

450

Williams Clough ②

400

350

300

Kinder Reservoir

←Water Treatment works

gate → bridge

N Continue here on return from [MAP 21]

gate → ←bridge

Landranger No. 110
Outdoor Leisure
Dark Peak

Tunsted Clough Farm

stile

STARTING AND
FINISHING POINT

car-park ①

MAP 20

To Hayfield

southerly direction, meandering through the peat and strangely-eroded boulders, to cross the head of Red Brook in ½ mile (800 m). A similar distance will bring you to the vicinity of Kinder Low. By keeping high up you should see the OS trig point and avoid being diverted down the slopes below Kinderlow End. The OS trig point is only a short way off the path, but can be tricky to find in mist. From Kinderlow there is a good view of Pym Chair on the skyline to the east. Now head just west of south for 300 yards (270 m) to Edale Rocks. Continue past Edale Rocks to drop down to the path which contours round Swine's Back. Ignoring the main eroded path down the hillside, which leads to Brown Knoll, continue

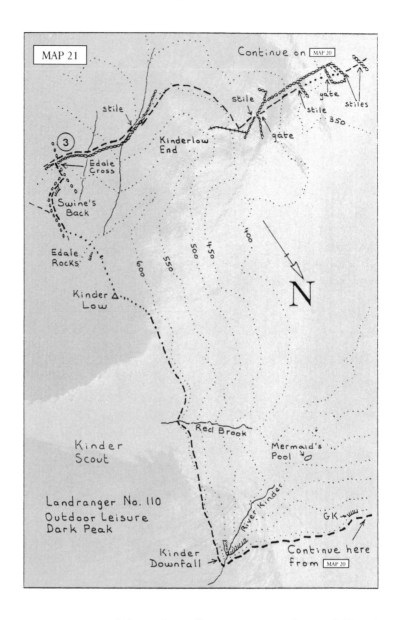

contouring round above the wall to meet a ruined sheepfold and then descend by the ruined wall to Edale Cross *(3)*.

Turn R onto the packhorse track and, after following it beside the wall for nearly ½ mile (800 m), turn R over a stile in the wall (PFS 'Hayfield via Tunstead Clough'). The conical-shaped hill to the south is South Head. Follow the path which contours round below Kinderlow End and ignore the L branch which seeks to divert you downhill. In ½ mile (800 m) a gate is reached. Don't go through the gate, but double back to cross a stile on the R. The gate immediately on the L leads to the first of

Opposite Path on the *northern side of Kinder Reservoir*

Kinder Reservoir

three fields, which are crossed at stiles and a gate to a main track. Follow the track down to a stile at Tunstead Clough Farm. Go straight ahead on the footpath, not through the farm, and join the farm road. In 250 yards (225 m) turn R onto the road, and walk back down this to Kinder Road and the car-park.

1 Kinder Trespass

For many years Kinder was barred to walkers, being preserved as a grouse moor for the privileged few. On Sunday 24 April 1932 the pent up emotions of the ramblers were released in the celebrated Kinder Scout Mass Trespass. Their intentions had been well advertised in the *Manchester Evening Chronicle* and some 400 people, avoiding the police who were waiting at the planned meeting point in Hayfield, assembled instead in the quarry to hear an address by Benny Rothman, the Mancunian leader of the Trespass. The police who had planned to arrest Benny at the railway station were thwarted when he arrived on his bike.

The Manchester Ramblers Federation opposed the idea of a mass trespass fearing that antagonizing the landowners would hinder rather than promote the cause of access. The walkers, however, set off along the road and up William Clough with the police in close attendance. As they climbed towards the Kinder Scout plateau, gamekeepers appeared and threatened them, but were unable to stop the advance. At the top they were met by more ramblers who had come over from Sheffield and Manchester by other routes, and a victory meeting was held before returning to Hayfield. At Hayfield, Benny and four others were arrested and taken to New Mills, where the next day they were charged with unlawful assembly and breach of the peace. Committed to the Derby Assizes on 21/22 July, they were found guilty of riotous assembly and Benny Rothman was sentenced to four months in prison.

The publicity, however, had made the public aware of the situation and restrictions were gradually lessened until in 1951 the formation of the Peak District National Park opened up the area with the negotiation of Access Agreements with the landowners. Now over 80 miles (20,737 hectares) of moorland are open to the public all year round, except for a few days each year kept for grouse shooting.

2 *William Clough*

The stream which tumbles down little waterfalls makes this a very pleasant approach to Kinder Scout (from the Saxon 'Kyndwr Scut' meaning 'water over the edge'). The stream, usually small but which after heavy rain becomes a torrent, has cut down through the peat exposing the layers of underlying shale and gritstone. The harder gritstone resists erosion and so causes the stream to flow in these pretty falls. Towards the top of the clough there is a thick deposit of clay covering the underlying rocks. This was formed in very cold conditions towards the end of the Ice Age. The runnels and scars are the work of water erosion.

3 *Edale Cross*

Recently protected and almost enclosed by a stone wall, this stone pillar in the shape of a cross is also called Champion Cross from 'Champayne' which was the name for the southern part of Peak Forest in the Middle Ages. The forest wards of Longdendale, Ashop, Edale and Champayne met near here, and such points were usually marked by a stone. This was an old medieval road and later a packhorse way. The initials J. G. and the date 1810 inscribed on the cross are much later and refer to restoration work.

2·15

LATHKILL AND BRADFORD DALES

STARTING AND
FINISHING POINT
Moor Lane car-park
near Youlgreave
(119-194645).

LENGTH
10 miles (16 km) or
8 miles (13 km)
variant

ASCENT
700 ft (210 m)

From its upper, narrow, dry limestone gorge, through the Derbyshire Dales Nature Reserve, where the river rises, to the green depths of the pools towards Alport, Lathkill Dale has always something of interest to see. At one time this tranquil valley was the centre of a major mining enterprise, with shafts and levels, waterwheels and aqueducts. The scene now is one of woods and flowers with the river flowing peacefully past, while the return along the River Bradford passes wide, deep pools where fish lie still in the depths.

Upper Lathkill Dale

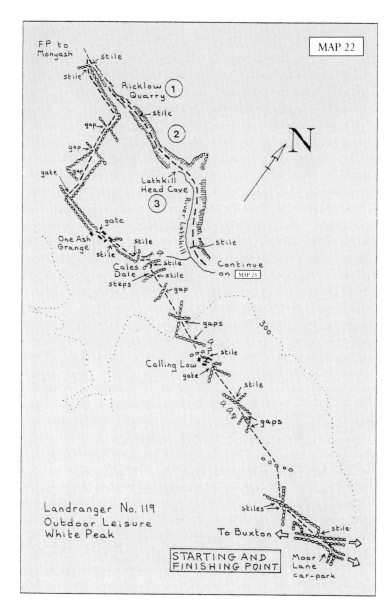

MAP 22

FP to
Monyash
stile

stile

Ricklow (1)
Quarry

stile

(2)

gap

gap

gate

Lathkill
Head Cave

(3)

River Lathkill

N

gate

One Ash
Grange

stile

stile

stile

Cales
Dale

stile

stile

Continue
on MAP 23

steps

gap

gap

gaps

300

stile

Calling Low
gate

stile

gaps

o o o

Landranger No. 119
Outdoor Leisure
White Peak

stiles

stile

To Buxton

STARTING AND
FINISHING POINT

Moor
Lane
car-park

ROUTE DESCRIPTION (Maps 22-24)

From the car-park turn L up to the road junction and over the
stile opposite. The waymarked path goes through a gap in the
wall and then over two stiles at the corner of the next field.
Head for the PFS at the ruined wall and turn half L towards the
trees. At the next gap turn half R and then through a gap into
the wood. Leaving the wood at a stile in about 50 yards (45 m),
go towards Calling Low Farm where a gate leads into the
farmyard. Go through two gates in the yard and a stile on the R
beyond the farm which leads to open fields. These are followed
downhill through three gaps to a stile above Cales Dale. A flight

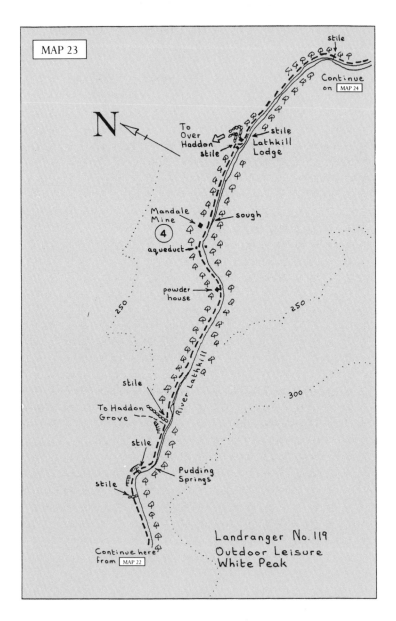

MAP 23

of 120 steep steps leads down into the bottom of the dale.

At the bottom, go over the stile where the walk may be shortened by a couple of miles by turning R down to Lathkill Dale. The longer route climbs ahead and then L (PFS 'Limestone Way') to cross a stile into a field, and then over high stone steps into the farmyard at One Ash Grange just to the L of a barn. Go through the yard and turn R by the camping barn to a gate onto the farm road which is followed up to a gate at the end on the R. The path now crosses four fields and turns L to descend to meet the head of Lathkill Dale at a stone stile. Turn sharp R over a wooden stile and walk down the dale, which rapidly narrows beneath Ricklow Quarry (1).

Reaching a stile, Lathkill Dale Nature Reserve *(2)* is now entered where the rare flower Jacob's Ladder may be found. In ½ mile (800 m), the obvious opening of Lathkill Head Cave *(3)* appears on the R and on the L is Parson's Tor, named after the Rector of Monyash who fell from the top with his horse in 1776 while returning in the snow after preaching at Bakewell. The junction with Cales Dale soon appears at a footbridge on the R. The waterfall of Pudding Springs ½ mile (800 m) further, tumbles over tufa beds, and then, at the site of Carter's Mill, the path enters ash woodland at a stile.

Signs of mining can be seen all down the valley for the next mile (1.6 km). Shortly after the pillars of the aqueduct, Mandale Mine *(4)* appears on the L with the sough just beside the path. A minor road is reached at a stile by Lathkill Lodge. Turn R and then L to pass the lodge. A further mile (1.6 km) beside wide fish pools (which have been artificially improved by weirs) will bring you to Conksbury Bridge. Turn R across the bridge on the old Grindleford turnpike, and a few yards up the hill turn L at a stile, now on the other side of the river. The path follows a fence and wall, crossing four stiles to Raper Lodge, where a small road is crossed. To the L is Coalpit Bridge, over which packhorses carried coal from Chesterfield. Continue beside a wall through eight fields to Alport, where the main road is joined at the bridge which dates from 1793. The Old Portway, an ancient trackway, forded the Lathkill at this point. The pretty village of Alport, with its attractive gardens, corn mill and old bridges, makes a pleasant detour.

Cross the main road and follow the track (PFS 'Middleton by Youlgreave') over the River Bradford and through a squeezer stile by a gate. The track runs beside the river to join another track just after a stile. Follow this track beside the river to a road and continue, now on the R bank. (In 1881 the River Bradford disappeared down a large hole caused by the collapse of old mine workings and reappeared at Darley Dale.) A ¼ mile (400 m) further at a stile, a flat stone slab bridge is crossed back to the L bank and through a small gate. Walk beside the river with its fish pools for ½ mile (800 m) to a small gate and turn R over the bridge. A track zig-zags up the hillside to the road. Turn R on the road, past Lomberdale Hall, and then L over the stile at the road bend to cross a field to a stile onto the higher road. Do not take the footpath opposite, but go L and then R over the next stile in a few yards where a clear waymarked path slants uphill across the field. At the third stile turn R, and follow the wall which leads back to Moor Lane car-park.

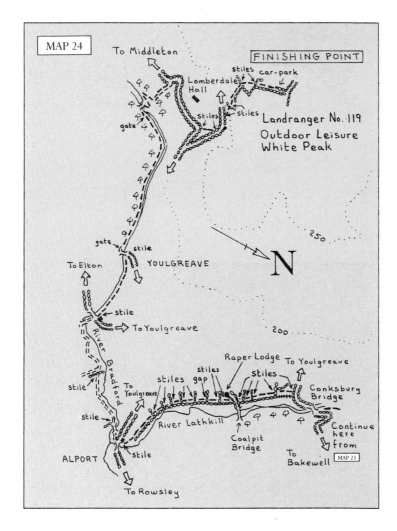

Continue here from MAP 23

1 Ricklow Quarry

The tips of the old marble mine have cascaded into the dale by an old mine entrance. The marble, a crinoidal limestone, was extracted from these workings until their collapse in 1900. The cave, a natural fissure, was enlarged by miners attempting to drain the Magpie Mine on Sheldon Moor, who after a short way found it intersected with a natural cavern. The short passage ends in a 15 ft (4.5 m) pitch, the total length of the cave being 250 ft (75 m). The date 1787 and the initials of Isaac Berresford (the miner who, together with his son, dug the Ricklow level) are carved at the entrance.

2 Lathkill Dale Nature Reserve

The dale, for so long ringing to the sounds of industry, is now a Derbyshire Dales Nature Reserve, managed by the Nature Conservancy Council; and the only noise comes from the visitors and the 10 000 school and university students who come to study here every year. The native ash woodland has

Opposite
Lathkill Dale

87

been actively managed from the eleventh century, and the river is claimed to be the purest in the country.

3 *Lathkill Head Cave*

If it has been wet weather the river may be flowing from the cave, but more usually it is dry and the river emerges further down the dale. The entrance, about 20 ft (6 m) high, soon closes down to a flat out crawl of 200 ft (60 m). The total length of the cave is 2000 ft (610 m), all of which floods in wet weather. Directly opposite, behind a bush, is Critchlow Cave which has 500 ft (150 m) of passages.

4 *Mandale Mine*

This is one of the oldest mines in Derbyshire having been worked from the thirteenth century and possibly from as far back as Roman times. Water has always been a problem with the mine. In 1798 the Mandale Mine Company started to drive the Mandale Sough, a task which took over thirty years. The sough can be seen where it emerges under the path and drains into the river. As this proved inadequate, pumping was found to be necessary and a 35 ft (10.5 m) diameter waterwheel was installed in 1840 for the purpose. The leat can be traced back along the hillside to the pillars of the aqueduct, which was constructed to carry the water across the river from the leat on the other side. The wheel pumped water out of the mine from a depth of 90 ft (27 m). In 1848 a Cornish beam engine was installed to improve the drainage of the mine, but the effort was in vain and the mine closed in 1851. The end wall of the engine house still stands and close by is the shaft which has been capped. The two small openings by the path are abandoned trial levels where no lead ore was found. On no account should mines be entered as there can be unstable rocks and hidden shafts.

THE ROACHES, LUD'S CHURCH AND GIB TORR

The Roaches and Back Forest, with the mysterious depths of Lud's Church, those strangest of naturalized English creatures – the wallabies–and one of the highest gritstone outcrops in the Peak, form a microcosm of all that is best in this area. Moorland and gritstone, heather and bilberries, the call of the lark

STARTING AND FINISHING POINT
Lay-by on the road between Upper Hulme, near Leek, and Roach End (119-004621).

LENGTH
10 miles (16 km)

ASCENT
1400 ft (430 m)

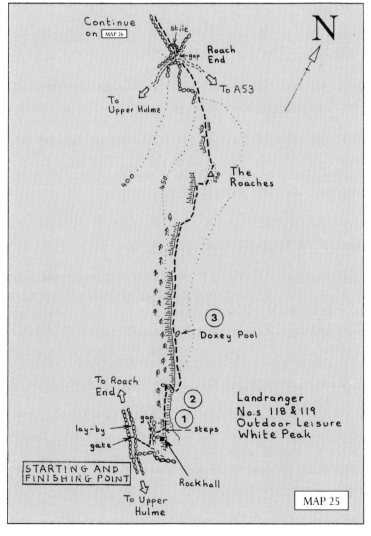

Continue on MAP 26

stile

Roach End

gap

To A53

To Upper Hulme

N

400

450

The Roaches

△

3

Doxey Pool

To Roach End

2

1

Landranger No.s 118 & 119
Outdoor Leisure
White Peak

lay-by

gap

steps

gate

STARTING AND FINISHING POINT

Rockhall

To Upper Hulme

MAP 25

89

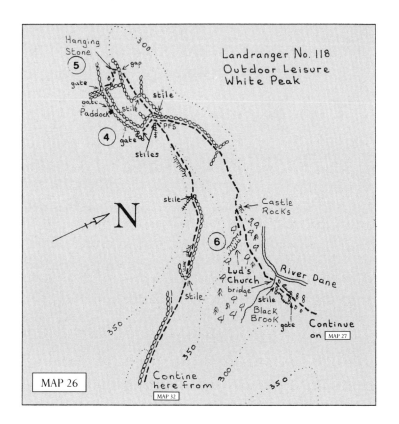

overhead, remind one of the quiet beauty of the northern moors. Yet the Roaches are so close to the road that on summer evenings the crags are busy with climbers enjoying some of the longest climbs in the Peak.

ROUTE DESCRIPTION (Maps 25-28)

Go through the gate next to the lay-by and follow the track towards the rocks with the slopes of Hen Cloud on the R ('Cloud' is from the Celtic 'clud' meaning 'hill'). Turn L and skirt Rockhall Cottage to turn R through a gap in the wall. A flight of rock steps leads up through the lower crags. These steps are the steepest and probably the hardest part of the walk! At the top on the L, perched on the edge of the vertical drop, is a gritstone boulder in the form of a seat or throne (1), and on the R is the Great Slab (2). Walk along the terrace and, on emerging from the trees, turn R along a broken wall. Ascend through a gap in the upper tier of rocks and at the top is moorland with fine views towards Ramshaw Rocks. Turn L along a clear path and Doxey Pool (3) is soon reached. Continue along the ridge to the summit of the Roaches.

Descending from the summit to the road at Roach End,

Opposite
The Roaches

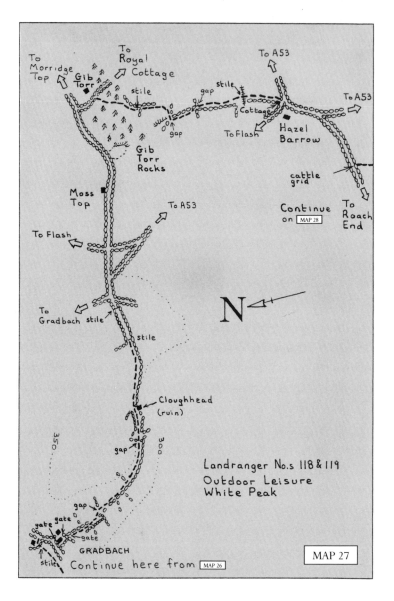

To Morridge Top

To Gib Torr

To Royal Cottage

To A53

To A53

stile

gap stile

stile

gap

Cottage

To Flash

Hazel Barrow

To A53

Gib Torr Rocks

cattle grid

Moss Top

To A53

Continue on MAP 28

To Roach End

To Flash

To Gradbach stile

stile

N

Cloughhead (ruin)

350

300

gap

Landranger No.s 118 & 119
Outdoor Leisure
White Peak

gap

gate gate

gate

GRADBACH

MAP 27

stile

Continue here from MAP 26

squeeze through the gap in the wall opposite and over a stile to follow the broad ridge of Back Forest. When the wall veers off to the L, continue on the concessionary path along the ridge. Cross the stile in the next wall and stay on the ridge, crossing another stile, until the path descends to meet a crossroads (PFS). Turn L over the stile towards Swythamley Hall *(4)* then R at the stile. Follow the lane which leads through two gates, passing Paddock Farm, until it turns L at a gate. Turn R on the concessionary footpath which is signed to Hanging Stone on the hill above. Ascend the rock steps on the L of Hanging Stone *(5)*, through a gap, and follow the path over the fields and three stiles to the Gradbach signpost.

The path soon enters woodland of silver birch, oak and

rowan, and arrives at Castle Rocks where a carved stone points the way to Lud's Church *(6)*. After exploring this, return to Castle Rocks and double back R to descend to where the River Dane meets Black Brook. Cross Black Brook by the bridge and, just uphill from the bridge, cross the wall on the L to follow a rising track through a gate and over the fields to a stile at the farm, which belongs to the Buxton and District Scouts. Turn R from the farmyard onto a road and in a few yards L again through a gate beside a farm. Passing through the farmyard and two gates follow a slightly sunken path, first on the R of the wall and then on the L. The prominent rock on the skyline to the L is called the Yawning Stone.

Make for the tumbledown Cloughhead Cottage by a tree and follow a rising track on the L side of the valley. At the top of the rise the view opens out with Gib Torr, the next objective, straight ahead. After two stiles, on emerging onto the road, note the unusual sign 'GRADBACH NOT ROACH END'. The depressions on the moor ahead are the remains of old coal pits. Keeping straight ahead, after ¾ mile (1.2 km) turn R and descend to Gib Torr Farm, just past which an unsigned path enters the woods on the R. On leaving the trees, pass through a stile and, avoiding the worst of the bog, make for just L of the huge gritstone tor on the skyline. Turn L through a gap and follow the ridge to a stile, and then emerge at the junction of three roads by a cottage.

Take the road opposite the cottage and then the R fork after the surprisingly situated Hazel Barrow (tropical) Fish Farm. In

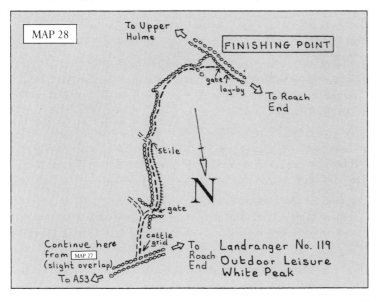

¼ mile (400 m) turn L at a cattle grid and follow the track to re-enter the Roaches Estate at a gate. When the track turns L, go over the stile to reach open moorland again. Cresting a slight rise, Hen Cloud reappears in view with Tittesworth Reservoir beyond. Descending the old pre-turnpike road, pass between Hen Cloud and the Roaches and walk down the track to the road.

1 *Gritstone Seat*

A throne is appropriate enough, for this was once the scene of a royal visit. A plaque nearby records 'Visited by the Prince and Princess of Teck August 23rd 1872'. The Princess of Teck was Queen Mary's mother and now, over a hundred years later, the area has passed into the hands of the Peak Park Board who bought it in 1980 for the sum of £185 000 after access difficulties had threatened this delightful area.

2 *Great Slab*

The Great Slab and the overhang above it is the route of the late Don Whillans' sensational climb, 'Sloth', which ascends directly over the overhang. On the face of the Great Slab is the Pedestal on which climbers may be seen summoning up courage to attempt the Sloth overhang, or perhaps on one of the easier routes which avoid the difficulties.

3 *Doxey Pool*

In summer this is a rippled pool set among heather, bilberry and cotton grass; in winter it can sometimes become a solid block of ice over which one walks almost without seeing it. There are no streams flowing into the pool, and it comes as something of a surprise to find that the summit of the Roaches is not far away, nor very much higher. Doxey Pool is supposedly named after the daughter of Bess Bowyer who lived at Rockhall and was herself the daughter of a highwayman.

4 *Swythamley Hall*

This was the home of Sir Philip Brocklehurst, and it was from near here that the most famous of the Roaches' inhabitants came. A zoo belonging to his brother released the wallabies which still roam the woods of Back Forest. Although the wallabies have been depleted in numbers by harsh winters, attempts have been made in recent years to maintain the stock by releasing others to join them. Their continued survival seems rather precarious, but by walking quietly and watching carefully, for they are so well camouflaged that unless they move it is difficult to see them, you may well take

home a very special memory of the Roaches. Please leave *Rockhall*
them to live quietly and do not disturb them, or in future
years, like the herd of deer which once also were to be seen
here, they may all have gone forever.

5 *Hanging Stone*

On one face of the Hanging Stone there is a memorial to Lt.
Col. Henry Courtney Brocklehurst. On the opposite face an
older testimonial reads:

Beneath this rock
August 1, 1874 was buried
BURKE
A Noble Mastiff
Black and Tan
Faithful as womar
Braver than man
A gun and a ramble
His heart's desire
With the friend of his life
The Swythamley Squire

6 *Lud's Church*

This is much easier to find since the Peak Park Board have
taken control of the area, but it was at one time a safe haven
for the Lollards who worshipped here. A short distance along
the path from Castle Rocks a narrow entrance on the R leads
you to a flight of steps descending into the bottom of Lud's
Church. This chasm, about 50 ft (15 m) deep, has been caused
by a landslip of gigantic proportions, and the main fault is
visible for some distance beyond Lud's Church. The name
Lud's Church is from the fourteenth-century pastor Walter
de Lud-auk, whose grand-daughter is supposed to have been
buried nearby after being killed in a raid by the King's troops.

95

3·17

BLEAKLOW FROM GLOSSOP

STARTING AND
FINISHING POINT
Old Glossop. Cars
may be parked
beside factory
(110-045948) on
the north-east
outskirts of
Glossop.

LENGTH
10 miles (16 km)

ASCENT
1450 ft (450 m)

There are three summits in the Peak District which achieve the magic height of 2000 ft (610 m) and two of these, Bleaklow Head and Higher Shelf Stones, are visited on this walk. The strangely eroded shapes of Wain Stones, Hern Stones and Higher Shelf Stones on the high moors have attracted walkers for over a hundred years.

The ascent, up Torside Clough, along the Pennine Way, and the descent, down the reputed Roman road of Doctor's Gate, both follow good footpaths beside clear, sparkling mountain streams. This ascent of Bleaklow is both delightful and much easier underfoot than many of the alternative routes.

ROUTE DESCRIPTION (Maps 29-31)

From the parking place, turn L at the end of the factory and follow the road round until it meets Charles Lane, which doubles back up the hill to a stile. Passing a quarry the sunken lane goes uphill through three stiles to a fourth where the walls fan out. Turn half L following the L wall, and in 250 yards (225 m) strike directly up the hillside to a stile in the fence. A bearing of NE brings you to Glossop Low Quarries (1), a complex array of depressions and spoil heaps through which you should attempt to navigate a straight line to arrive at the OS trig point on the top of Cock Hill.

From the summit walk for about ½ mile (800 m) still on a NE bearing over rough grass and heather until a stony track is reached. Turn R along it to the ruined shooting cabin on Glossop Low. From the ruin follow a faint path, again heading NE, and in a few yards the Woodlands Valley comes into view. On the skyline are the twin Holme Moss television masts, and opposite can be seen Crowden Youth Hostel in the valley of Crowden Brook, which is for many walkers the end of a long, first day on the Pennine Way. The path leads across the moor for ¼ mile (400 m) until, quite suddenly, Torside Clough appears at your feet. The Pennine Way is joined at this point.

Opposite
*The Pennine Way
looking towards
Higher Shelf Stones*

96

Turn R and follow Clough Edge on a level path, with the clough gradually climbing to meet it. After a mile (1.6 km) Wildboar Grain joints Torside Clough. Turn L, descending to cross the stream, and follow the path eastwards up the L bank. In ¾ mile (1.2 km), where the stream gradually disappears and the peat groughs become more evident, the path swings gradually R. Continue along the path and after a further ¼ mile (400 m) the cairn on Bleaklow Head is reached, surrounded by a sea of silver sand.

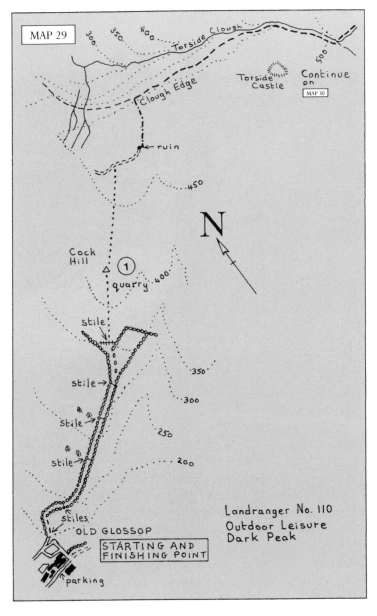

Continue on MAP 30

MAP 29

Landranger No. 110
Outdoor Leisure
Dark Peak

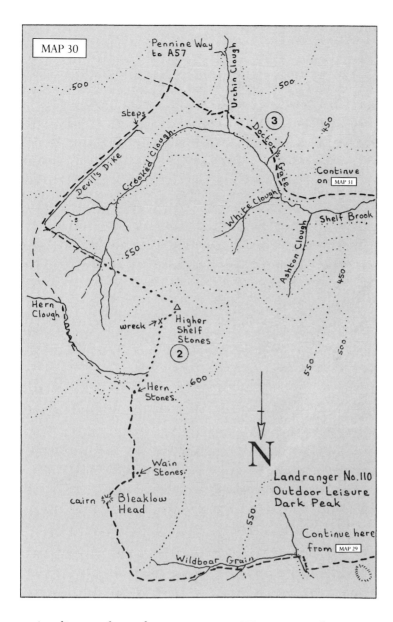

MAP 30

A solitary pole to the SW points to Wain Stones (known as 'The Kiss'), just out of sight but only 200 yards (180 m) away. From here in clear weather Hern Stones will be seen due S less than ½ mile (800 m) distant. The intervening ground is without a clear path although very many feet tread this way every weekend; the reason for this is the peat.

At Hern Stones the Pennine Way is left temporarily in order to visit Higher Shelf Stones (2), the second of the 2000 ft (610 m) summits. This is reached after approximately ½ mile (800 m) on a SW bearing, but by aiming just L of the direct line to Higher Shelf Stones the wreckage of a Flying Fortress aircraft may be visited first.

The escarpment to the SW is Lower Shelf Stones with Glossop beyond, while Shelf Brook flows through the deep valley ahead. Now head SE towards a dyke near the head of Crooked Clough. Climb up this to rejoin the Pennine Way which follows Devil's Dike (probably an old boundary ditch). Turn R and in ½ mile (800 m) a flight of wooden steps is met at the end of a board walk built to minimize erosion. In ¼ mile (400 m) turn R at a crossing path (Doctor's Gate) *(3)* and descend past Urchin Clough to follow Shelf Brook towards Glossop (once known as Glott's Valley).

When the valley flattens out, a further ½ mile (800 m) brings you to the Memorial Footbridge across Shelf Brook. From here the boundary of open country lies ¾ mile (1.2 km) downstream where a track is joined coming in from the R by a barn. Go down this track to cross a stile and over the bridge ahead. The track is now followed through a gap and three gates; the last opens onto an unmetalled road which leads in ½ mile (800 m) back to Old Glossop.

1 Glossop Low Quarries

This quarry, which closed towards the end of the nineteenth century, was used as a source of local building stone, specializing in paving flags and roofing slabs. A rood of roofing slabs was 44 square yards (37 sq m) and cost 52 shillings at the quarry and 64 shillings in the town when the quarry was in its heyday.

That the lane which leads up to the quarries on Cock Hill once took substantial traffic is evident from the gritstone paving slabs which may still be seen where they have not yet been covered by encroaching grass.

2 Higher Shelf Stones

This is typical Bleaklow; wild peat groughs (though not as deep as those of Kinder), no path and only the compass to guide you. In bad weather this is quite a frightening place to be; in good weather it is a fascinating area to visit. Bleaklow comes from the Old English meaning 'dark coloured hill'.

Very close to the OS trig point the remains of a Flying Fortress may be seen. The gleaming metal is scattered over a wide area almost as though the accident had only just happened; in fact the crash, in which thirteen American airmen died, occurred on 3 November 1948. Four engines and many metal fragments are scattered about and, although it is illegal to remove any pieces, at one time the entire fuselage and tail could be seen.

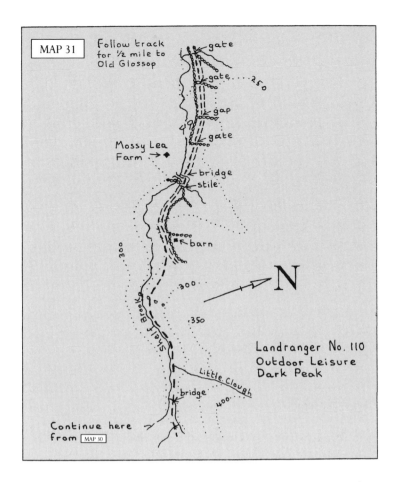

MAP 31

Follow track for ½ mile to Old Glossop

gate

gate.... 250

gap

gate

Mossy Lea Farm →◆

bridge

stile

barn

300

300

350

Shelf Brook

N

Landranger No. 110
Outdoor Leisure
Dark Peak

Little Clough

bridge

400

Continue here from MAP 30

The rocks at Higher Shelf Stones are covered more than usual in graffiti, including an early example dating from 7 October 1871.

3 Doctor's Gate

Gate means road and since 1627 this track has been known as Doctor Talbotes Gate. Dr John Talbot, Vicar of Glossop, 1494-1550, was the illegitimate son of the Earl of Shrewsbury and may have used the old Roman road when visiting his father's castle in Sheffield. The Roman road, from the fort of Navio at Hope to that of Melandra at Glossop, led via Hope Cross, across Blackley Clough, past Hayridge Farm and Oyster Clough to the Snake Road. The next section over Coldharbour Moor, is the best preserved and shows how the road was constructed with slabs set on edge between kerbstones. As the track descends Shelf Brook, it becomes very eroded and loses its character. The road was used by packhorses until the construction of the turnpike in 1821.

CROWDEN BROOK TO RUSHUP EDGE FROM EDALE

STARTING AND
FINISHING POINT
Edale car-park
(110-124853).

LENGTH
10 miles (16 km)

ASCENT
1650 ft (500 m)

Crowden Brook makes an interesting way up onto the Kinder plateau, and it is often almost deserted when Grindsbrook is bearing its usual heavy weekend traffic. The strangely eroded stones of the plateau are among the most fascinating of sculptured shapes. The walk encircles the upper Edale Valley which is well seen both from the approach via Upper Booth and from Rushup Edge, a favoured spot for hang-gliders.

ROUTE DESCRIPTION (Maps 32–34)

From the car-park, walk under the railway bridge and up the road towards Edale village *(1)* to the Old Nag's Head which is reached in about ½ mile (800 m). Turn L (PFS 'Upper Booth and Hayfield') to pass through a kissing gate and then over a stile. The sunken track is followed beside a small stream for 300 yards (270 m), and at the PFS ('Hayfield via Upper Booth and Jacob's Ladder') turn L over the stile. Crossing the narrow field, turn R on the far side and walk up the hedgeside to a stile in the corner. Climbing gradually uphill through a series of three stiles, the path flattens out. On the L are the upper reaches of the Edale Valley with Rushup Edge on the far side and Brown Knoll at its head. The prominent notch in the far skyline just to the R of Mam Tor, through which the road to Edale passes, is known as Mam Nick.

The path continues through a further four stiles, descending to turn R at a stile onto an old track. Walk down the track to the hamlet of Upper Booth ('Booth' is the Tudor word for a temporary shelter used by herdsmen). On reaching Upper Booth the track turns L and then immediately R to a stile into the farmyard. Going through the farmyard out onto the road, turn R downhill for a few yards to a bridge. Turn R over the stile and follow the bank of Crowden Brook, crossing a stile and then up to a barn. Go over the stile and cross Crowden Brook at the

*Opposite Rushup
Edge from Mam Tor*

102

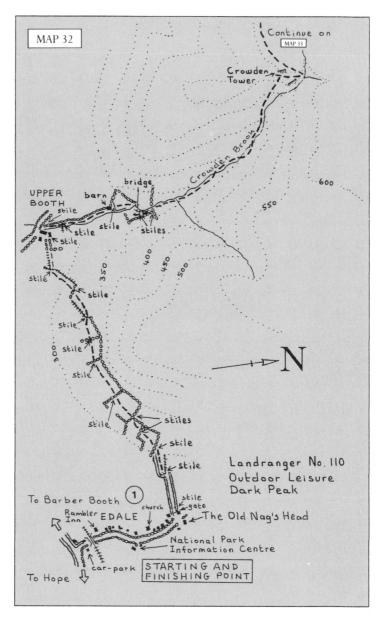

footbridge. Cross another stile, turn L, and at the next stile the boundary of open country is reached.

The route follows Crowden Brook all the way up to the Kinder plateau high above, crossing and re-crossing it several times as the path gradually steepens. When Crowden Tower looms overhead, climb L to just below the rocks. Turn R and contour round to join the head of Crowden Brook. The alternative direct route up the waterfalls is great fun, but only if you are experienced in rock scrambling.

104

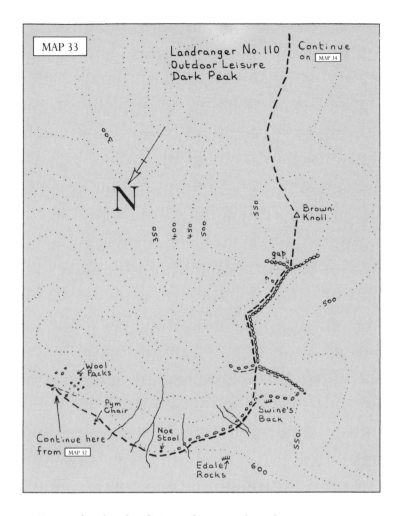

MAP 33

Landranger No. 110
Outdoor Leisure
Dark Peak

Continue on MAP 34

N

Brown Knoll

gap

Wool Packs

Pym Chair

Noe Stool

Swine's Back

Continue here from MAP 32

Edale Rocks

From the head of Crowden Brook, where two streams tumbling down over the bare grit bedrock join, the path turns L to follow the edge. In about ½ mile (800 m), an area of strangely eroded rocks, known as the Wool Packs, is reached. After examining these rocks, which indeed look like bundles of fleeces awaiting collection, head for Pym Chair, the prominent, saddle-shaped rock on the skyline. The path actually skirts Pym Chair, but it makes a good excuse for a stop and a lot of the point of the walk is lost if you hurry past these rocks. The highest point in the Peak District at 2088 ft (636 m) is just north of here. Continue along the wide, and in wet weather boggy, path to Noe Stool, another prominent rock overlooking the headwaters of the River Noe which flows down to join the Derwent near Hathersage. Ahead across the next dip is Swine's Back, a prominent escarpment, and high on the R is Edale Rocks. Following the path beside the broken wall, turn L at Swine's Back and descend to cross the old packhorse route to Hayfield which comes up from Jacob's Ladder on the L. Go up the slope

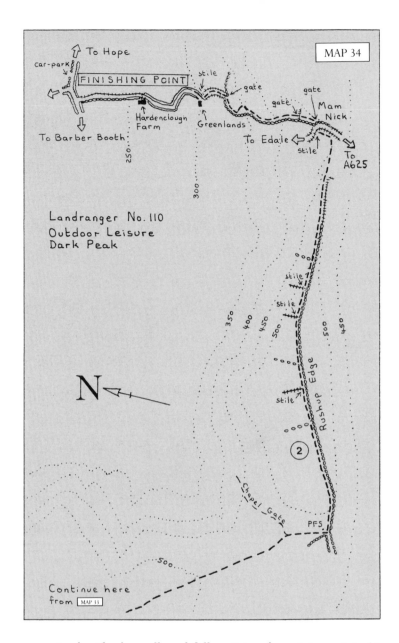

MAP 34

To Hope

car-park

FINISHING POINT

stile

gate

gate

gate

Mam
Nick

Hardenclough
Farm

Greenlands

To Barber Booth

To Edale

stile

To
A625

250

300

Landranger No. 110
Outdoor Leisure
Dark Peak

N

350 400 450 500

500 450

stile

stile

Rushup Edge

stile

2

Chapel Gate

PFS

Continue here
from MAP 33

500

opposite, beside the wall, and follow it to where it turns R in ¼ mile (400 m). In another ¼ mile (400 m), at a gap at the junction with a wall coming in from the L, leave the wall and aim SSE towards the unseen OS trig point of Brown Knoll which appears shortly.

Brown Knoll summit to Rushup Edge is about 2 miles (3.2 km) across wild moorland with few landmarks. The general direction to head is SE. A wide path, more or less boggy according to the conditions, will assist, and the air shaft of the 2 mile (3.2 km) long Cowburn railway tunnel provides one useful reference point, until eventually the old Chapel Gate packhorse

Opposite
The Wool Packs

way is met coming up from Edale on the L (Chapel refers to Chapel en le Frith). Turn R on to this track and in 200 yards (180 m) (PFS) turn L onto the Rushup Edge path. Climb gradually now towards Rushup Edge *(2)*, and ½ mile (800 m) past the PFS a fence is crossed at a stile and the highest point is reached. From here the route is all downhill. Ahead is the Great Ridge, which stretches from Mam Tor to Lose Hill, and in the far distance is Win Hill. The path descends, crossing two stiles, continuing on the ridge to the very end where a sharp L turn leads to a stile at Mam Nick.

Go almost straight across the road to a gate. Follow the wall downhill through a gate, and in ½ mile (800 m) go through another gate onto a fence-lined path which leads to Greenlands, where the road is joined at a stile. In ½ mile (800 m) the metalled farm road comes out on to the main valley road close to the car-park which is just up the road to the R.

1 Edale Village See page 57

2 Rushup Edge

On the other side of the wall is an ancient trackway, still a right of way, but not often used, which was sensibly constructed out of the wind a few feet down on the lee side to protect the jaggers on this exposed route. Modern walkers, preferring the view, now stick to the crest. Lord's Seat, the highest point, boasts a Bronze Age burial mound, but usually it is the hang gliders which attract one's attention as they soar in the upcurrents of the edge or swoop in low to land.

Away to the R is the large limestone scar of Eldon Hill Quarry. There is a constant battle in the Peak District, as elsewhere, between the preservers of natural beauty and the developers. Eldon Hole, reputedly bottomless, in fact about 250 ft deep (75 m), is a natural pothole on the same hill and the largest open chasm in Derbyshire.

The hummocks and mounds on the slopes facing Edale may look like the spoil heaps of a quarry, but they are in fact the result of landslips, caused by repeated freeze and thaw action on the steep ground. The effect is, of course, most pronounced on this north-facing slope which holds the snow in winter and casts long shadows over the Edale Valley. Farms in the valley will therefore be found on the north side in order to make the best of the sunshine. There is also a marked east-west difference in climate: Jacob's Ladder, at the head of the valley, is very much wetter than the eastern end of the dale, receiving as much as 10 in (254 mm) more each year.

3·19

FROGGATT EDGE, BURBAGE EDGE AND PADLEY GORGE

The popular climbing grounds of Froggatt and Curbar Edges are thronged with climbers at weekends. White Edge, which has no cliffs, is quiet by contrast, and has only recently been opened to the public since its acquisition by the Peak Park Board. Longshaw Estate is crossed to Burbage Edge, another popular climbing area, and the walk passes beneath the crags to give a view of the climbs. Higger Tor and the hill fort of Carl Wark are visited, and finally the charmingly wooded Padley Gorge completes this circuit of the edges.

ROUTE DESCRIPTION (Maps 35–38)

Leave the car-park at the far end from the entrance, over the stile and down to the stream. Climbing up to a gate, turn R onto

STARTING AND FINISHING POINT
Hay Wood car-park, near The Grouse Inn, on the B6054 Calver to Dronfield road (119-256778).

LENGTH
13 miles (20 km) or 10 miles (16 km) variant

ASCENT
1150 ft (360 m)

Froggatt Edge

the road and shortly L through a gate at the boundary of open country. Walk along a broad track of silver sand for about ½ mile (800 m) to a kissing gate. In 200 yards (180 m) Stoke Flat Stone Circle is just off the track to the L. The track continues along Froggatt Edge and then Curbar Edge to descend in 1½ miles (2.4 km) to a kissing gate at Curbar Gap.

Turn L on to the road and in 50 yards (45 m), on the R of the entrance to the small car-park, go over the stile by a guide stone. Go straight ahead, ignoring the L fork, to cross Sandyford Brook at the wooden bridge. Continue beside the wall, which

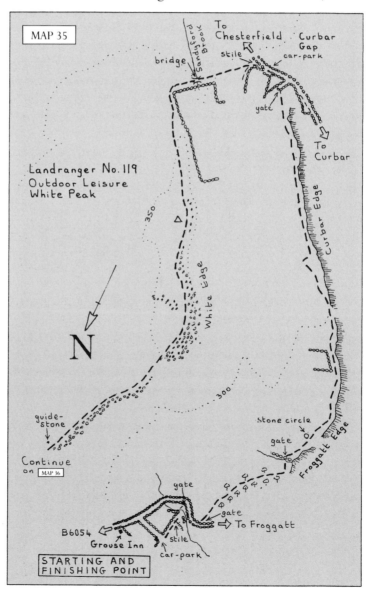

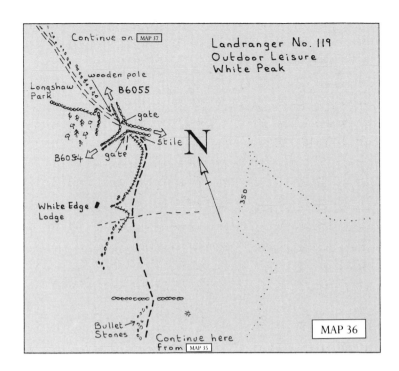

Continue on MAP 37

Landranger No. 119
Outdoor Leisure
White Peak

wooden pole

Longshaw
Park

B6055

gate

stile

N

B6054

gate

White Edge
Lodge

350

Bullet
Stones

Continue here
from MAP 35

MAP 36

soon bends L, and up onto White Edge. The route is clearly waymarked and in ½ mile (800 m) passes the OS trig point. After 1¼ miles (2 km) the only significant outcrop of rock on the edge is passed. These pock-marked rocks are called Bullet Stones as they were used for target practice during the last war. Go through the wall and across the moor, until a fence is met with White Edge Lodge below on the L. The fence leads down by snow fencing to a stile, and a gate leads you onto the B6054 at a three way junction.

Go straight across the road junction and through the gate by the sign 'Wooden Pole' to follow the main grassy track through the estate and into the wood at a gate. Skirting Longshaw Lodge (1), turn R along the drive to the gate onto the B6521. Go almost straight across to a gate, through the woods for 300 yards (270 m), and then fork R up to the road at a stile. The shorter variant turns L here to the Toad's Mouth.

The wide track opposite leads through a gate and then runs beneath Burbage Rocks for about 1½ miles (2.4 km). At the end go through the gate onto the road, turn L across the bridge and then L again over the stile. In a few yards take the R path which rises gradually and ¾ mile (1·2 km) of easy walking brings you to Higger Tor. Ahead across the dip is the wall flanking the Iron Age hill fort of Carl Wark (2), which is reached by a descent followed by a short ascent. From the old entrance to the fort on the south-west side, a path descends towards Burbage Brook, but about 100 yards (90 m) before the stream take a small path

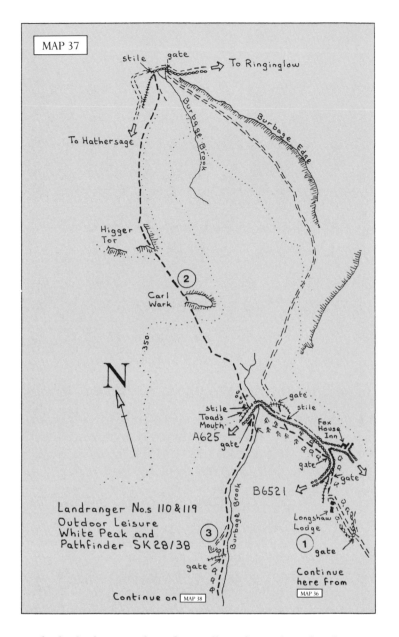

MAP 37

R which climbs onto the ridge. Follow the rocky ridge down to the road at a stile by the Toad's Mouth Rock, only the eye of which is artificial.

Turn R along the road for a few yards and then L through a little gate into the National Trust estate. Follow Burbage Brook down to meet the woods in about ½ mile (800 m). Just before entering the wood there is a quarry track which leads to a small quarry containing several millstones (3) tumbled about among the rocks. Return to follow Burbage Brook as it descends Padley Gorge, where further millstones may be seen beside the path. Going through a new gate, the path descends gradually for about ½ mile (800 m); when it starts to rise again, don't go L down to the brook, but stay up, and the path soon continues its descent to emerge from the trees in a clearing. Turn R in front of the stone waterworks building and over a stile in the fence to follow a small path through the bracken. The path joins a fence behind the houses and then runs beside a stone wall which soon turns L and descends to the track. The ravine on the R, where the path joins the track, is the Bole Hill quarry incline *(4)*. Turn L on the track beside Padley Chapel *(5)* and walk past the station and over the railway bridge. A path just to the R of the café now leads up to the main road. Go straight across (sign 'No Through Road') and up the hill for 300 yards (270 m) to turn L at the second of the two footpaths. This leads uphill through a gate into a wood and in ¼ mile (400 m) a stile is reached into the car-park.

1 Longshaw Lodge

The 1600 acre (650 hectare) Longshaw Estate belongs to the National Trust. The Lodge was built in 1827 as a shooting lodge for the Duke of Rutland. An information centre, shop and cafeteria open at weekends throughout the year and on some other days. The sign 'Wooden Pole' at the entrance to the estate refers to a guide post on the Dronfield to Tideswell packhorse track.

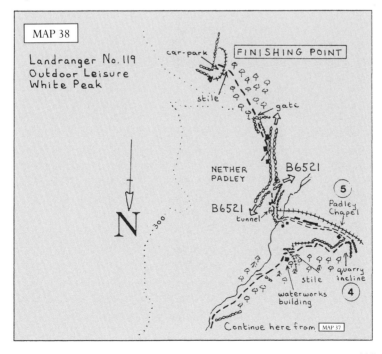

MAP 38

Landranger No. 119
Outdoor Leisure
White Peak

car-park

FINISHING POINT

stile

gate

NETHER PADLEY

B6521

B6521
tunnel

Padley Chapel

5

N
300°

quarry incline

stile

4

waterworks building

Continue here from MAP 37

2 *Carl Wark*

This isolated rocky knoll is, like its companion Higger Tor, formed of hard gritstone, the softer surrounding rock having weathered away. It forms a natural defensive position of about 2 acres (0.8 hectares). Fortified on its north side by a 10 ft (3 m) high wall of substantial boulders, it is thought to be an Iron Age hill fort, though some authorities put it later at post-Roman, fifth or sixth century. The original entrance lies at the south-west corner where there is an information plaque and a stone trough.

3 *Millstones* See page 22

4 *Quarry Incline*

Over one million tons of stone, extracted from Bole Hill Quarries, was used in the building of the Derwent and Howden Reservoir dams commenced in 1901. The stone was loaded onto waggons in the quarry, pulled by engines to the top of this incline, and then lowered by gravity under the control of cables which pulled up empty waggons. The incline passed under the track to join the railway, and, as the trucks were standard gauge, they could be transferred directly to the main line.

5 *Padley Chapel*

This Roman Catholic chapel is the private chapel of Padley Hall. When in 1588 two Jesuit priests were found hiding there, they were taken to Derby where they were hung, drawn and quartered. An annual pilgrimage is held here on the last Thursday in July in their memory. After being used as a cowshed, and then to house the navvies who dug Totley railway tunnel, the chapel was rededicated in 1933.

Opposite and above Hathersage Moor

4·20

DERWENT AND HOWDEN CIRCUIT

STARTING AND
FINISHING POINT
Fairholme car-park
by the dam of
Derwent Reservoir
(110-173893).

LENGTH
21 miles (34 km)

ASCENT
2200 ft (670 m)

This high level circuit of the Derwent Reservoir's watershed covers some of the wildest and most remote moors in the Peak District. It is a tough walk even in good summer weather and should be attempted only by experienced walkers who know how to use map and compass. Try to pick dryish conditions as it is much harder going when the ground is very wet. Usually only a few people will be seen once the high moors have been reached and, with just the grouse and larks for company and rough moorland grass and heather underfoot, the splendid solitude has a very special appeal.

ROUTE DESCRIPTION (Maps 39–45)

From the car-park walk down to beneath the dam and then up the path which doubles back to join the main track beside the Derwent Reservoir *(1)* at a stile. After 1½ miles (2.4 km) easy walking beside the reservoir, and just before the Howden Dam, turn R (PFS 'Bradfield and Strines'). A clear path is followed high on the south side of Abbey Brook (the land belonged to Welbeck Abbey in the twelfth century) and in just under 2 miles (3.2 km) passes Berristers Tor. The path bends R to Sheepfold Clough, where the faint remains of shooting cabins are still just visible. Cross Sheepfold Clough and descend L to cross Abbey Brook. Then, on a faint path which peters out, climb above Foul Clough onto the plateau. Turn L, crossing the upper part of the clough, and follow the edge, where the going is easiest, to Wet Stones, and from here head NW to pick up the clear path which goes N along Howden Edge. The OS trig point on Margery Hill is about 1¼ miles (2 km) along the edge, but set back from it and so is easy to miss. From the OS trig point a path leads in ¼ mile (400 m) to cross Cut Gate, the old packhorse route from the Woodlands Valley to Penistone, and from here it is ¾ mile (1.2 km), marked by occasional boundary stakes, to the second OS trig point which is on Outer Edge.

The next 3½ miles (5.5 km) to Swains Head are wild country

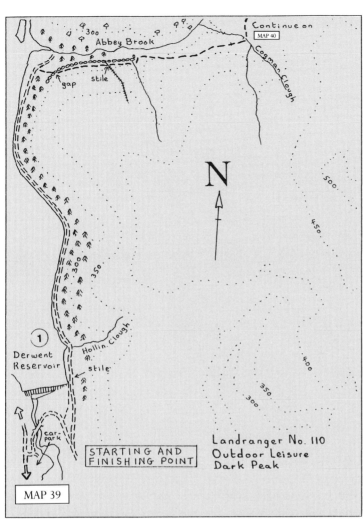

MAP 39

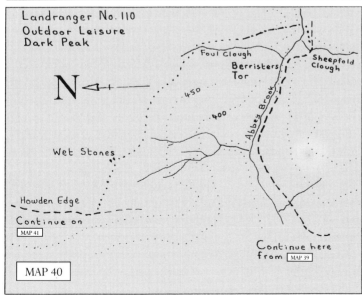

MAP 40

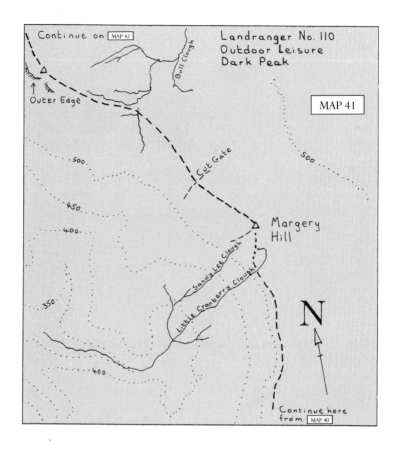

with few landmarks, but a path has developed in recent years which aids navigation and progress. An isolated gritstone block, with the date 1894 carved on top, is passed just before Swains Head, which is marked only by a small stake and a path which branches off R. Continue for 50 yards (45 m) and then turn L down a clough (no path) to meet the infant River Derwent. Follow this upstream for ⅓ mile (530 m) on a faint path and then climb beside, or in, the clough which leads up onto the plateau (again no path). Continue in the same direction, through the strangely carved rocks of Barrow Stones to the Crown Stone, a very large boulder overlooking the Westend Valley ahead. A path now follows the edge SW to Grinah Stones in ½ mile (800 m) and from here a clear path sets off towards Bleaklow Stones. It is easy to get diverted from the proper route as there are several minor paths, but by taking the upper path if in doubt, Bleaklow Stones is reached in 1 mile (1.6 km).

Go past Bleaklow Stones for about 300 yards (270 m) and then head due S down the ridge (no path). Although there are faint paths over the moor it is easy to lose them, and care is

*Opposite Moors
below Margery Hill*

118

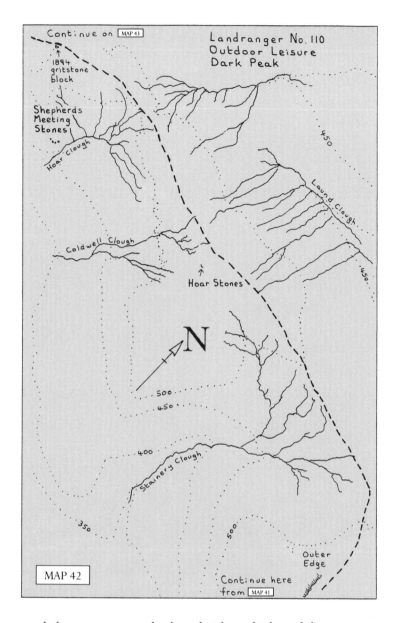

Continue on MAP 43

Landranger No. 110
Outdoor Leisure
Dark Peak

1894
gritstone
block

Shepherds
Meeting
Stones

Hoar Clough

Coldwell Clough

Laund Clough

450

450

Hoar Stones

N

500
450

400

Scanery Clough

350

500

MAP 42

Outer
Edge

Continue here
from MAP 41

needed to remain on the broad ridge which undulates over a
minor top for over 2 miles (3.2 km) to the OS trig point between
the Westend and Alport Valleys. The path then becomes clearer
and soon gives good views down into the Alport Valley (2) on
the R. In 1 mile (1.6 km) a wall is reached and followed to the
cliff edge overlooking Alport Castles. Take care as the drop is
steep and unexpected. The path now gives easy walking for 2
miles (3.2 km) until, as a wall comes in from the R, a ladder stile,
followed shortly by another, brings you out at a major track
junction of a hollowed packhorseway paved with small stones.
Turn L and descend gradually to a gate at Lockerbrook Farm.
Two hundred and fifty yards (225 m) past the farm turn R at a

120

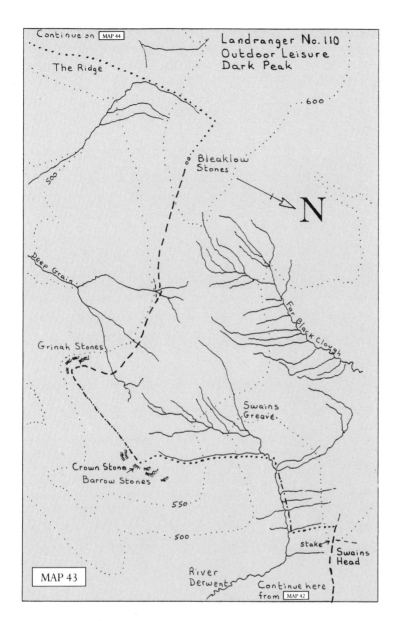

Continue on MAP 44

Landranger No. 110
Outdoor Leisure
Dark Peak

The Ridge

600

Bleaklow
Stones

N

500

Deep Grain

Grinah Stones

Far Black Clough

Swains
Greave

Crown Stone
Barrow Stones

550

500

MAP 43

stake

Swains
Head

River
Derwent

Continue here
from MAP 42

gap (PFS 'Forest Walk to Fairholme') and go down to enter the wood at a stile. A path leads down through the trees, over the leat at a bridge, and out onto the road opposite the car-park.

1 Derwent and Howden Reservoirs

The high local annual rainfall, which exceeds 50 in (1270 mm) a year, together with the deep valley which narrows to provide good sites for dams, led to the early exploitation of the Derwent Valley for the benefit of Sheffield, Derby, Leicester and Nottingham. The construction of these masonry dams 115 ft (35 m) high, which taper from 178 ft (54 m) thick at the base to 10 ft (3 m) at the top, was begun in 1901 and

121

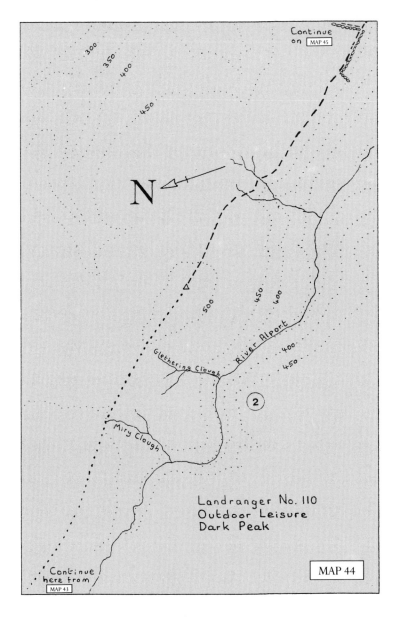

Continue on MAP 45

N

River Alport

Glethering Clough

500

450 400

400

450

2

Miry Clough

Landranger No. 110
Outdoor Leisure
Dark Peak

MAP 44

Continue
here from
MAP 43

300
350
400
450

continued for the next fifteen years. Workmen and their
families were housed in temporary dwellings which, with
school and shops for the thousand inhabitants, became known
as 'Tin Town'. The massive amounts of stone for the dams,
which were over 1000 ft (300 m) long and built in Gothic
style, was quarried at Bole Hill Quarries (see page 115),
carried by rail to Bamford and then, via a specially built
railway, to Birchinlee on the west side of the valley.

In 1986 a fly past here commemorated the famous Dam
Busters who practised over these dams for their epic flight to
bomb similar dams in the Ruhr Valley during World War II.
The film of their mission was also shot using this location.

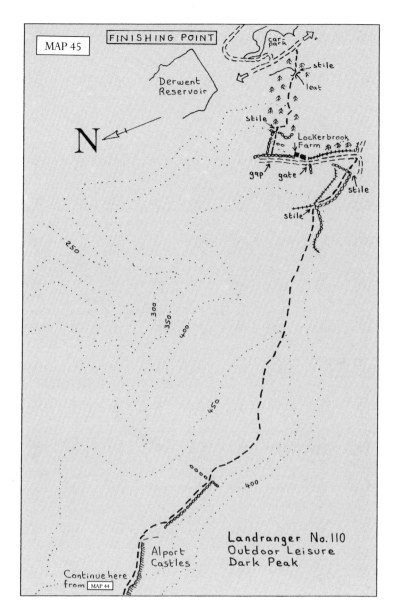

MAP 45

FINISHING POINT

Derwent
Reservoir

car park

stile

leat

stile

Lockerbrook Farm

stile

gap   gate   stile

stile

N

250

300

350

400

450

400

Landranger No. 110
Outdoor Leisure
Dark Peak

Alport
Castles

Continue here
from MAP 44

2 Alport Valley

The traffic on the busy A57 rushes past the foot of Alport
Dale, yet only 5 miles (8 km) up the valley is Grains in the
Water, one of the most remote, quiet and, for lovers of
solitude, most attractive dale heads in the Peak District. It is
seen at its best as you walk back from Bleaklow high on the
rim of the deep, steep-sided valley, in the late afternoon sun,
or finest of all by moonlight.

Alport Castles, in the lower part of the dale, is a landslip of
gigantic proportions where a veritable mountain of gritstone
rock has slid towards the valley on its underlying bed of shale.

123

APPENDICES

ACCESS FOR THE WALKER

The name National Park is misleading as it is not in fact owned by the nation. Most of the land is in private ownership and right of access only applies to public footpaths or where Access Agreements have been made with the land-owners.

The National Parks and Access to the Countryside Act 1949 required the County Council to provide a definitive map showing the public rights-of-way. Inclusion on this map is proof that a right-of-way exists. These are classified as public footpaths or as public bridleways.

There are however other large areas within the Park, known as Access Land, where unrestricted access is permitted.

ACCESS AGREEMENTS

The National Parks and Access to the Country-side Act 1949, as amended by the Countryside Act 1968, makes the Peak Park Joint Planning Board responsible for making arrangements with the landowners for the public to have access to open, uncultivated land, including mountain and moorland. 'Access' means the right to wander at will over the land for open air recreation and is not confined to specific routes. At the present time Access Agreements cover over 80 square miles (20,737 hectares) of open country. It must be remembered, however, that the land remains in private ownership and provides sheep grazing and grouse moorland.

SHOOTING SEASON

Each Access Agreement includes a clause allow-ing each moor to be closed to public access on up to twelve days each year during the grouse shooting season (12 August–10 December). Lists of dates when the moors will be closed are published monthly for August, September and October. These lists are available from the Board about a fortnight in advance and are also dis-played on notices around the area. These notices include a map which shows access moors numbering each shooting area. When specific moors are closed to public access for the day, a sign to this effect is also displayed. There is no shooting on Sundays and hence all access areas are open on Sunday.

THE NATIONAL TRUST

The policy of the National Trust is to give free access at all times to its open spaces; however there cannot be unrestricted access to tenanted farms and to cetain ecologically sensitive areas. The National Trust owns land on Kinder and Bleaklow, which are covered by Access Agree-ments, and also land to the east of the River Derwent, as well as Longshaw Country Park and Lyme Park.

CONCESSIONARY PATHS

There are a number of permissive or concession-ary paths in the Peak District. These are marked in red on the Outdoor Leisure maps and are usually signposted and waymarked. Although they are generally open for public use, they are not rights-of-way and the landowner retains the right to close them.

SAFETY

The walks described in this book cover a very wide range of difficulty, from short, easy strolls which can be completed in virtually any weather conditions at any time of the year, to those which should only be attempted by fit and experienced walkers with considerable knowledge of moun-tain and moorland navigation.

Despite the lack of really high mountains (only three tops scrape over the height of 2000 ft (610 m) which justifies mountain status), the

Peak District provides some very tough challenges. The weather is notorious for its changeability, from good visibility to dense mist, from mild conditions to arctic temperatures, and from a gentle breeze to a strength-sapping gale. Rescuers in the Peak District are called out to about forty incidents each year and, while some are unavoidable, most of these would not have occurred if people had taken sensible precautions.

DO
Ensure you have the right equipment.
Wear boots if there is any rough ground to be covered, for a firm grip.
Take waterproof and windproof clothing.
Take spare warm clothing, especially during the winter.
Carry an ample supply of food with emergency rations saved until the end of the day.
Carry a map and compass and know how to use them.
Obtain a weather forecast before you set out.
Leave word of your intended route with someone, and remember to tell them when you are safely back.

DON'T
Go alone on the high moorland unless you are very experienced.
Leave any member of the party behind on the walk.
Explore old mine shafts and workings.

A booklet *Safety on Mountains* is published by the British Mountaineering Council and is available from Peak District National Park Information Centres or by post from the Peak Park Joint Planning Board.

GIVING A GRID REFERENCE

The starting and finishing point of each walk in this book is identified by a six-figure number, called a grid reference, coupled with the number of the appropriate Landranger map. This is a simple way of uniquely identifying any point on an Ordnance Survey map.

Grid lines are the thin lines which run vertically and horizontally across the map at 1 kilometre intervals and are shown on the

Landranger (1:50 000). Pathfinder (1:25 000) and Outdoor Leisure (1:25 000) OS maps. Each line is numbered at the edge of the map (and sometimes at intervals across the map as well) with a number in the range 00 to 99. The 00 lines make larger squares with sides of 100 small squares, representing 100 kilometres. These larger squares are identified by two letters. The entire network of lines covering the British Isles, excluding Ireland, is called the National Grid.

The example below shows how to find the grid reference for the OS trig point on the map shown in fig 3.

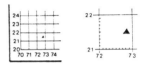

FIGURE 3 Giving a grid reference

Step 1
Find the number of the grid line to the *left* of the point. In the example this is 18.
Step 2
Estimate the number of tenths of a square that the point is from this grid line and append this number to the first. In the example this is 9, so now we have 189.
Step 3
Find the number of the grid line *below* the point and append this number to the ones above. Here the number is 95, so we have 18995.
Step 4
Estimate the number of tenths of a square that the point is from this grid line and append this last number. In the example it is 7, so we have 189957. This is called a six-figure grid reference and when the sheet number of the map is also given it identifies a place to within 100 metres.

A full grid reference also includes the identification letters of the appropriate 100 km square of the National Grid.

COUNTRYSIDE ACCESS CHARTER

Your rights of way are:
* public footpaths – on foot only;
* bridleways – on foot, horseback and pedal cycle;
* byways (usually old roads), most 'roads used as public paths' and, of course, public roads – all traffic.

Use maps and signs – Ordnance Survey Pathfinder and Landranger maps show most public rights of way – or look for paths that have coloured waymarking arrows – yellow on footpaths, blue on bridleways, red on tracks that can be legally used by vehicles.

On rights of way you can:
* take a pram, pushchair or wheelchair if practicable;
* take a dog (on a lead or under close control);
* take a short route round an illegal obstruction or remove it sufficiently to get past.
You have a right to go for recreation to:
* public parks and open spaces – on foot;
* most commons near older towns and cities – on foot and sometimes on horseback;
* private land where the owner has a formal agreement with the local authority.

In addition:
You can use the following by local or established custom or consent – ask for advice if you're unsure:
* many areas of open country like mountain, moorland, fell and coastal areas, especially those of the National Trust, and most commons;
* some woods and forest, especially those owned by the Forestry Commission;
* country parks and picnic sites;
* most beaches;
* towpaths on canals and rivers;
* some land that is being rested from agriculture, where notices allowing access are displayed;
* some private paths and tracks.
Consent sometimes extends to riding horses and pedal cycles.

For your information:
* county and metropolitan district councils and London boroughs have a duty to protect, maintain and record rights of way, and hold registers of commons and village greens – report problems you find to them;
* obstructions, dangerous animals, harassment and misleading signs on rights of way are illegal;
* if a public path runs along the edge of a field, it must not be ploughed or disturbed;
* a public path across a field can be ploughed or disturbed to cultivate a crop, but the surface must be quickly restored and the line of the path made apparent on the ground;
* crops (other than grass) must not be allowed to inconvenience the use of a right of way, or prevent the line from being apparent on the ground;
* landowners can require you to leave land to which you have no right of access;
* motor vehicles are normally permitted only on roads, byways and some 'roads used as public paths';
* follow any local bylaws.
And, wherever you go, follow the country code:
* enjoy the countryside and repect its life and work;
* guard against all risk of fire;
* fasten all gates;
* keep your dogs under close control;
* keep to public paths across farmland;
* use gates and stiles to cross fences, hedges and walls
* leave livestock, crops and machinery alone;
* take your litter home;
* help to keep all water clean;
* protect wildlife, plants and trees;
* take special care on country roads;
* make no unnecessary noise.

This Charter is for practical guidance in England only. It was prepared by the Countryside Commission.

Addresses of Useful Organizations

British Mountaineering Council,
Crawford House,
Booth Street East,
Manchester, M13 9RZ

Addresses of hill-walking clubs available on enclosure of a stamped, addressed envelope.

The Camping and Caravanning Club
Greenfields House,
Westwood Way,
Coventry, CV4 8JH
Tel (0203) 694 995

Council for National Parks,
246 Lavender Hill,
London, SW11 1LJ
(071) 924 4077

Countryside Commission,
John Dower House,
Crescent Place,
Cheltenham,
Gloucestershire, GL50 3RA,
Tel Cheltenham (0242) 521 381

The Long Distance Walkers Association
117 Higher Lane,
Rainford,
St Helens,
Merseyside, WA11 8BQ
Tel St Helens (0744) 882 638

Losehill Hall,
Peak National Park Study Centre,
Castleton,
Derbyshire, S30 2WB
Tel Hope Valley (0433) 620 373

The National Trust,
36 Queen Anne's Gate,
London, SW1H 9AS.
Tel (071) 222 9251

The National Trust
(Regional Office for the Peak District)
East Midlands Regional Office,
Clumber Park Stableyard,
Worksop, S80 3BE
Tel Worksop (0909) 486411

English Nature,
Manor Barn,
Over Hadden,
Bakewell, DE45 1JE
Tel (0629) 815 095

Peak District National Park,
Aldern House,
Baslow Road,
Bakewell,
Derbyshire, DE4 1AE
Tel Bakewell (0629) 814 321

Peak Park Conservation Volunteers,
(0629) 815 185

Ramblers' Association,
1/5 Wandsworth Road,
London, SW8 2XX
Tel (071) 582 6878

Youth Hostels Association (England and Wales),
Trevelyan House,
8 St Stephens Hill,
St Albans,
Hertfordshire, AL1 2DY
St Albans (0727) 855215

INDEX